JESUS AS A TEACHER

JESUS AS A TEACHER:

A MULTIDISCIPLINARY CASE STUDY

J.T. DILLON

University of California

Wipf & Stock

PUBLISHERS

Eugene, Oregon

Wipf and Stock Publishers
199 W 8th Ave, Suite 3
Eugene, OR 97401

Jesus as a Teacher
A Multidisciplinary Case Study
By Dillon, James T.

ISBN: 1-59752-268-6
Publication date 6/20/2005
Previously published by International Scholars Publications, 1995

TABLE OF CONTENTS

LIST OF TABLES

PREFACE

How may we understand Jesus as a teacher? This book proposes a way of understanding this famous historical teacher. The understanding is based on a study of all aspects of his teaching, examined in light of what is known from scholarly research in two fields--New Testament (studies on Jesus), and Education (studies on teaching). It is a multidisciplinary case study of Jesus as a teacher.

Each chapter answers one main question about one main aspect of teaching. There is first of all the question about the teacher. Who was Jesus? (chapter l). Jesus was a Jewish religious teacher in Palestine around the year 30 A.D. What did he teach, and why? (chapter 2). His subject was "The Kingdom of God" and his aim in teaching it was "Repent!"

Where and when, or in what circumstances did Jesus teach? (chapter 3). This is the question of milieu, the conditions surrounding teaching. Jesus taught anytime and everywhere, in all manner of places and occasions, but always within Jewish milieux, as if the Greco-Roman society around him did not exist. Whom did he teach? (chapter 4). He taught all kinds of Jewish people--the elite and the outcaste, women and men, urban and rural, wealthy and poor.

How did Jesus teach? This question describes the activity of teaching, the methods Jesus used to teach people. He taught them "The Kingdom of God" first of all by actions (chapter 5) and then by words (chapter 6). Both his conduct and his language were parabolic and actional, teaching people the activity that constituted his subject matter (Kingdom of God) and also teaching the activity that was his aim for their learning (Repent). Action was what he taught, and action was how he taught it.

Who learned what from the teaching? or, what was the result? (chapter 7). As far as can be seen, few of the people whom Jesus taught learned much of what he was teaching them. After his death great numbers of people came to learn a great deal, but not from Jesus and not what he taught. They learned something else taught by somebody else. Not many people learned as a result of Jesus' teaching.

That describes Jesus as a teacher. The final question and chapter evaluates the quality of his teaching. How well did Jesus teach? How good of a teacher was he? (chapter 8). Jesus was an accomplished teacher -- yet a demonstrably ineffective one.

Taken together, these interrelated questions and answers form an understanding of Jesus as a teacher. The questions are answered by taking into account what is known about Jesus and about teaching from various scholarly disciplines in fields of Education and New Testament studies; and by taking into account other studies on Jesus the teacher over the past one hundred years. In more technical terms, these points refer to the problem for study, the method used to study it, and the research literature already published on the topic. All of that is described in the Appendix, "The Study of Jesus as a Teacher." The Appendix is written in general, non-technical language so that any interested reader--not just specialists and scholars--can learn such things as how this study was conducted, what sources were used, and so forth. Some readers will find it helpful to start with the Appendix, others to end with it, while others can perfectly well read and appreciate the book without the Appendix at all--for the book stands on its own and the reader already knows enough from this Preface.

The conclusions of this study may seem odd or unsatisfying or even objectionable. That is the way they work out. Not a lot is known about Jesus, especially the historical Jesus; and a lot remains to be known about teaching, especially good teaching. Both are interesting topics, and together they make a fascinating case for study. It is also a most perplexing case to study. For other purposes, though--not for study--it is an easy matter to know and tell about Jesus. That is another kind of knowledge than is pursued in this study.

This book is a multidisciplinary case study of the famous historical teacher, Jesus of Nazareth. It proposes what I now think is the most reliable answer to the question, How may we understand Jesus as a teacher?

- J.T. Dillon

Chapter 1

THE TEACHER

Jesus was a Jewish religious teacher in Palestine around the year 30 A.D. The question of who the teacher is comprises both the person and the pedagogue: Who was Jesus as a person or individual character; and, who was he in the character of teacher?

Historical Character

The origins of Yehoshua or Jesus, also called at the time Jesus of Nazareth (e.g., Mk 10.47), are Jewish, religious, and Galileean. He first appeared as one among the people in the religious movement of a local prophet, John the Baptist, accepting John's message of repentance in face of God's coming judgement and participating in a public immersion or baptism in the Jordan River (Mk 1.9). Thereafter Jesus appeared as a religious teacher in Galilee (Mk 1.14).

Galilee, a province in Palestine to the north of Jerusalem, is the place of Jesus' birth and life activity. He was born a few years before the calculated start of this present era, at a time when rule over Galilee was passing from Herod the Great (died 4 B.C.) to Herod Antipas under sufferance of the Roman Emperor Augustus (died A.D. 14). In that place and time but within Jewish milieux Jesus lived, growing up in Nazareth and residing for a time as an adult in Capernaum on the northern shore of Lake Galilee (Lk 4.16; Mk 2.1).

Jesus came from a large family, headed by his father Joseph and mother Miriam or Mary, with two or more sisters and four other brothers -- Jacob or James, Joses or Joseph, Judas, and Simon (Mk 6.3; Lk 4.22). These but not Jesus married and left children (cf. I Cor 8.5). By the time he had begun to teach, Jesus' father had died or otherwise ceased to figure. The rest of his family publicly disapproved of his conduct as a teacher, regarding him as demented or otherwise needing to be taken in hand (Mk 3.21, 31). Not among his followers while he lived, his mother and brothers counted in that company after Jesus' death (Acts 1.14), especially his brother James. James became their recognized leader in Jerusalem, more prominent than even Jesus' very closest disciples while he lived and taught (Gal. 2.9; Acts 21.18). Thirty years later (62) James was executed, as his brother had been and before him John the Baptist -- James by the Jewish mode of stoning, Jesus by the Roman mode of crucifixion, and John by the Herodian mode of decapitation.

Jesus' education presumably followed the forms customary to a Jewish youth. As an adult he could read Hebrew aloud (Lk 4.16), and he showed himself well versed in Jewish traditions and ritual, law and scriptures. But as a teacher he had no formal training or education and he wrote nothing. He may incidentally have picked up some Greek from the intensively Hellenized world about him in Galilee, including neighboring towns and people, Jews and non-Jews, who spoke Greek commonly, but his world was Jewish and his tongue Aramaic, not a trace of Hellene or Roman about him. Before becoming a teacher, Jesus had worked as a carpenter (Mk 6.3), thereafter being supported by various groupings of people who accepted him as a teacher and who accompanied him as he went about teaching (Lk 8.3).

Having emerged in Galilee, Jesus ended in Jerusalem to the south, in Judea, after teaching here and there in the environs for a year or more. Because his death coincided with the great national festival of Passover (Mk 15.6), it can be fixed to a Friday in April, the 7th in the year 30 (or the 3rd, in 33). Jesus had come to this city -- the religious, national, historical, political, social center of Judaism -- with some followers and companions, as had also the Roman prefect of Judea, Pontius Pilatus, together with a cohort of auxiliary troops to reinforce the garrison in anticipation of the crowds and disorders then customary. On some criminal count (civil disorder or threat?), Jesus was arrested and executed by the Roman authority in the mode customary for criminals, crucifixion (Mk 15.15) -- that is, by being transfixed upright to a wooden tee so as gradually to asphyxiate over some days' time, in public view.

Beyond that, nothing is known of Jesus' life and person. What is known are these awkward particulars, forming no story and no portrait, nor any biography either as bios or ethos. Rather the particulars are known in the manner of disparate bits and pieces of some lost mosaic, without any conception of the whole which they are to form and into whose frame they can be placed as related if scattered components. They are pieces without the puzzle.

(Apart from New Testament sources cited, the particulars recounted and not counted here rely on studies by Bornkamm, 1974; Conzelmann, 1973; Dillon, 1982; Jeremias, 1971. The alternative date for the crucifixion is from Humphreys & Waddington, 1983; details of crucifixion are described in Hengel, 1977. Some 2000 *Life of Jesus* works are listed in a recent bibliography by Kissinger, 1985, of which all but a handful may be regarded as uninformative about the life of Jesus.)

Among things about which particulars are no longer even known are Jesus' appearance and physique, youthful experiences, growth and development, emotional make-up, lifestyle, preferences, everyday habits and mannerisms, foibles and shortcomings, private opinions, aspirations, struggles, and moods, secret vices and virtues, public comings and goings, sequence of events, places, times, and people, traits and complexes of idiosyncrasy, temperament and character, career and personality -- in short, everything today thought most noteworthy of a person, especially one in the public eye. To the extent that Jesus' contemporaries could so much as have noted such things, they did not chronicle them. Jesus did not speak of himself and he wrote nothing at all down, while no contemporary account or record took any notice whatsoever of Jesus, neither hide nor hair. Jesus was not famous. Most people in the know never had occasion to meet or so much as to hear of him.

On the other hand, to the extent that Jesus was noted at the time, he like anyone in that milieu, was known not for person and personality but for place and role. Jesus was known as a teacher. As a teacher he was known by his actions and words. The character of Jesus, including his personality such as it was, does not inform his actions and words, as if lying behind these, but is defined by them.

Little is known of Jesus' life and person, and of that even less is known in detail. Jesus was known in his character as a teacher. Here there is detail enough, and complete coherence.

Character as Teacher

As with any individual who teaches, Jesus can be understood in his character as teacher in addition to personal or private character. In Jesus' case, as with any other in his time but not in ours, an understanding of the individual emerges primarily from his status and function in the milieu. Jesus is known in his character as teacher.

Depiction as Teacher

As depicted in the gospel texts, Jesus' actions and words characterize him as a teacher. What he does is seen to constitute teaching. Table 1 gives a sampling of those depictions that explicitly identify him as *teacher* and his activity as *teaching*. There are many more such explicit mentions in the texts, some 40 in all; many explicit mentions of other teacher-related terms, e.g., explaining, disciple; all manner of depictions of teaching without explicit mention of such terms, e.g., telling parables, answering questions, pronouncing on law; and the depiction in the text as a whole (Baird, 1969; Stein, 1978; Robbins, 1984). Table 1 offers for convenient reference only a sample, and a sample only of those depictions that use the words teacher and teaching.

At issue here is not everything about Jesus as a teacher but only his character *as* a teacher. In this character Jesus is seen to interact with learners over subject matter in circumstance. His activity is depicted *as* teaching, and people are seen to address him *as* teacher (Table 1).

All manner of people address Jesus as a teacher, approaching him with requests, laying disputes for him to settle, exhibiting infirmities for him to heal, asking for direction, probing his attitudes and knowledge, and engaging him in disputations over points of law and conduct. Each of these was customary at the time in address to a teacher.

Table 1. Depiction of Jesus as *Teacher*

Activity as Teaching	Address as Teacher
1. "Jesus and his disciples came to the town of Capernaum, and on the next Sabbath Jesus went to the synagogue and began to teach. The people who heard him were amazed at the way he taught, for he wasn't like the teachers of the Law; instead, he taught with authority" (Mk 1.21-22).	1. " 'Teacher, I brought my son to you, because he has an evil spirit in him and cannot talk ' " (Mk 9.17).
2. "Again Jesus began to teach beside Lake Galilee. The crowd that gathered around him was so large that he got into a boat and sat in it. The boat was out in the water, and the crowd stood on the shore at the water's edge. He used parables to teach them many things" (Mk 4.1-2).	2. " 'Good Teacher, what must I do to receive eternal life? ' " (Mk 10.17).
3. "Then Jesus left that place, went to the province of Judea, and crossed the Jordan River. Crowds came flocking to him again, and he taught them, as he always did" (Mk 10.1).	3. " 'Teacher, there is something we want you to do for us ' " (Mk 10.35).
4. "Then Jesus sent two of them with these instructions: 'Go into the city [Jerusalem], ... and say to the owner of the house: "The Teacher says, Where is the room where my disciples and I will eat the Passover meal?" ' " (Mk 14.13-14).	4. " 'Teacher, I want to see again ' " (Mk 10.51).
5. "A Pharisee invited Jesus to have dinner with him, and Jesus went to his house and sat down to eat. ... 'Simon, I have something to tell you.' - 'Yes, Teacher,' he said, 'tell me ' " (Lk 7.36,40).	5. " 'Teacher, ... Tell us, is it against our Law to pay taxes to the Roman Emperor? Should we pay them or not? ' " (Mk 12.14).
6. "As Jesus and his disciples went on their way, he came to a village where a woman named Martha welcomed him in her home. She had a sister named Mary, who sat at the feet of the Lord and listened to his teaching" (Lk 10.38-39).	6. " 'Well done, Teacher! It is true, as you say, that ... ' " (Mk 12.32).
	7. " 'Teacher, tell my brother to divide with me the property our father left us ' " (Lk 12.13).
	8. " 'Teacher, I am ready to go with you wherever you go ' " (Mt. 8.19).
	9. [to disciples] " 'Why does your teacher eat with such people? ' " (Mt. 9.11).
	10. [to disciples] "Does your teacher pay the Temple tax? ' " (Mt. 17.24).
	11. '"Teacher, which is the greatest commandment in the Law" ' " (Mt 22.36).

All manner of settings -- all Jewish -- are depicted for his teaching activity. He teaches in synagogues on the Sabbath, in homes, and outdoors as well, such as in a boat on the lakeshore. He goes out and about, teaching in villages, towns, and cities of Galilee and Judea, such as Capernaum and Jerusalem. He teaches individuals, groups, crowds of ordinary people, elite people such as Pharisees, marginal types such as women and the sick, and disreputable types such as sinners. He has followers and companions, and disciples who serve as agents and messengers. He teaches in actions and words, such as parables, in a manner that strikes people as self-authoritative. Not all of this activity was customary for a teacher at the time.

In all of these respects of address and activity, Jesus is characterized as a teacher. On some of these counts he was also seen as distinctive in that character.

Distinction as Teacher

Jesus' distinction is here understood quite apart from eminence or excellence, on grounds of the differences between him and others in their shared character as teacher. One way to understand this particular teacher is to appreciate how he differed from the teachers of his day, and from teachers of the present day.

Significant differences were noted by people at the time. They remain singularly distinctive to the discerning eye of today (as that of Bornkamm, 1960; Jeremias, 1971; Robbins, 1984). Above all, people saw Jesus' actions and words as *self-authoritative*, in striking contrast to other teachers (Mk 1.22). He did not expound or cite others as authority or support but said and did things of his own assertion. For example, his characteristic speech ran "Amen, I tell you that..." by contrast to the customary "Thus saith the Lord/Prophets/Law" or "Thus it is written," then followed by "amen!" (Schweizer, 1971). Indeed, Jesus never represented himself as instructed by God to do or to say anything that he said and did, nor represented any of his teachings as insight into God's secret ways, intimate revelations, visions or the like -- nor even as the product of his own years of special searchings or meditations which might ground his assertions in deed and word. He was known to have had no formal education and to be the pupil of no known teacher; he lacked theological study, ordination, and office. People criticized Jesus on this count, for teaching without authorization (Mk 6.2), and officials challenged his authority to teach (Mk 11.27).

Other differences much remarked at the time (and today by Bornkamm, 1960; Jeremias, 1971; Stanton, 1974) noted the kind of people whom Jesus taught. Some of these, including some of his disciples, were people whom religious teachers would never accept as pupils nor in any way even teach--such as women. What is more, they included types of people that religious teachers sought positively to avoid in all respects of life, not alone teaching--disreputable types such as notorious sinners against the law, and outcasts such as despised and immoral tax-collectors. Jesus was vividly criticized and taunted on these accounts (e.g., Mk 2.15-16, Mt 11.18). He was cited as well for other conduct unbecoming a religious teacher, such as laxity of religious observance (e.g., Mk 2.18, 24, 7.5).

Further distinctive features of Jesus' character as teacher could not have been overlooked in view of their contrast with customary modes of teaching (Bornkamm, 1960; Vermes, 1973; Wilder, 1971). He was seen to teach elsewhere than in synagogues and other places designated for teaching; to teach otherwise than by sitting and receiving pupils for instruction; and to teach also in public to anyone rather than only in private to associates and intimates. His speech and manner were direct and immediate rather than aloof and remote; informal and unsystematic rather than ritualized and codified; pressing, insistent, and affrontive rather than deliberate, cautious, and polite.

Special distinction attached to Jesus' relations with those who were his disciples or pupils (Blinzer, 1971; Conzelmann, 1973; Schweizer, 1971). Above all, Jesus attached disciples to himself whereas disciples attached themselves to a teacher. Always the individual would offer to be a disciple of some teacher, never would the teacher call; always it is Jesus who chose the individual to be a disciple. Further unlike other teachers, Jesus did not gather a closed group of disciples about him and did not assemble their group before him in some hall, there to hear lectures, hold discussions, and study the law. Jesus' disciples were not his partners in any such activities, putting questions and raising objections; and they were not themselves to become teachers independently of their teacher--as would a former pupil of some famous rabbi or scribe.

As for schoolteachers of today, the same differences apply in training, activity, place, time, and pupils. What is more, a complex of differences and similarities relates the three sets of teachers--Jesus, teachers of his day, and schoolteachers of today. The differences that distinguished Jesus from the teachers of his day also serve to differentiate him, perhaps more sharply, from those of today.

Certain similarities between Jesus and the teachers of his day distinguish them from today's teachers. Other features shared by teachers of today and Jesus' day, but not by Jesus, serve to further distinction. All of these go towards understanding Jesus in his character as teacher.

Obvious differences distinguish all of today's teachers from all teachers of Jesus' day, including Jesus. These would include, for almost all established states of the 20th-century world, gross differences in all aspects of milieu, ways of thinking and acting, extent of schooling in society, and place of religion in both school and society. Even in the first century of this era, Judaic Palestine was acutely recognized and treated by all concerned as an outstandingly special case among all the bizarre collectivities of the known world. Today it is enough to appreciate that schoolteachers are in the main not Aramaic-speaking Jews in Palestine, not to say in the first century A.D.

To appreciate the complex of particular differences a reverse method can be followed, characterizing today's schoolteachers in their own positive terms. These terms will then serve to identify features that did *not* characterize Jesus as a teacher, including those characteristics shared by teachers of his day and today but not by him. All such features for all teachers can systematically be located within the common categories of teaching.

Teacher. Schoolteachers of today are trained through some years of formal study both of subject matter and pedagogy, including some supervised practice. They are then certified, licensed, and commissioned to teach under authority and regulation of the state, the society, and the subject-matter specialists. Of themselves teachers hold no authority and possess no special knowledge. Their personality may permissibly enter to enliven their role and function but otherwise must be kept to themselves, statutorily at a remove from the persons whom they teach.

Subject matter & aim. School subjects are universally academic, systematized and codified bodies of knowledge or skill that are to be apprehended by cognitive processes, in particular the intellectual. Feelings and other personal matters, such as the way one chooses to live, are in particular not at issue as subject or objectives of school or society.

Learner. Learners everywhere are select people so designated for purposes of teaching. They are children, youth and other subordinates, compelled *en masse* to receive teaching and identified for that purpose by age-graded groups (they are "5th graders" or "secondary students"). Selected aspiring learners may later become teachers independent of those who taught them, but like their teachers dependent on authorization. Neither learner nor teacher is autonomous.

Milieu. Teaching proceeds only at that special time and place designated for it, at private remove from all other events (school, classroom, periods, ages).

Activity. Teaching is ritualized in procedure, language, and behavior. Participants act out set-pieces with known, invariant roles and clear beginnings, endings and intermissions. The activity is primarily verbal and propositional, a transmission and reception of codified information derived from an external source--a text, a personage, a body, a doctrine, a research, a medium--to whose authority reference, citation, and appeal is made at every step in the preparation, presentation, and evaluation of teaching. Teaching proceeds primarily by telling, and learning by re-telling, of things authorized to know.

Insofar as these terms characterize schoolteaching today, they serve to describe *by contrast* the character of Jesus as a teacher.

The character of teacher is the same, the terms in which it is exhibited and played out differ. Jesus' character too can be understood within the same categories but in other, contrasting terms; so also may other past and certain present teachers be understood. In Jesus' case, the teacher was autonomous, knowledgeable but untrained and unauthorized. The subject and aim were religious and actional, not secular and intellectual. The learners were adult anybodies, not youthful designates. The milieu was publicly anywhere, not only by assignation of place and time. The activity consisted of actions as well as words, not verbal acts alone, which were parabolic in form and interactive-responsive in dynamic, rather than propositional and expository-recitative.

It is in terms such as these that Jesus can be understood as a teacher--and incidentally too, as a personality. That goes to answer the generic question of who the teacher is. Next the specifics of these terms in Jesus' case will be detailed through each of the remaining categories common to teaching--what he taught and why, where and when, to whom, how, and with what result. Considered in relation with one another and together in relation to other teachers, these questions and answers will yield knowledge of Jesus as a teacher.

Chapter 2

SUBSTANCE OF THE TEACHING

What did Jesus teach, and to what end? "The Kingdom of God is at hand. Repent!" (Mk 1.15; Mt 4.17)

Subject matter and aim here form complements, for being actional: something is happening; act in accordance. The matter is not academic. It is not constituted of a set of factual or notional propositions. Neither "Kingdom of God" nor "Repent" finds suitable place within the curricular contents and objectives common in schools. But they can nonetheless be made over into the object of academic instruction, conveying to students a body of knowledge to the end that they cognize, appreciate, and apply it. That is not the kind of subject and aim of Jesus' teaching. "Kingdom of God" is an activity, and "Repent" is an activity.

Subject: "Kingdom of God"

Jesus formulated the subject of his teaching as the Kingdom of God, and gave other expression to it in form of actions and parables. The formula is found in 60 separate sayings of his, recorded in all sources, here set out for convenient reference in Table 2.

The thematic subject of his teaching is that the Kingdom of God is coming soon:

> The right time has come, and the Kingdom of
> God is near! (Mk 1.15; Mt 4.17)

Table 2. "Kingdom of God" (K) Sayings in the Synoptic Gospels*

MARK		LUKE ONLY		SOURCE COMMON TO MATTHEW & LUKE		MATTHEW ONLY	
1.15	K is near	4.43	good news of K	L6.20	K is yours	5.10 13.38	K belongs
4.11	secret of K	9.60	proclaim K	7.28	in K	5.19ab, 8.12, 13.52, 18.1, 18.4	in K
4.26, 4.30	K is like	9.62	no use for K	10.9, 11.2, 11.20	K comes	5.20, 7.21, 18.3, 21.31	enter K
9.1	K come	10.11, 17.20, 21.31, 22.18	K comes	12.31	be concerned with K	13.19	message about K
9.47, 10.23, 10.24, 10.25	enter K	12.32	be concerned with K	13.20	K is like	13.43	their Father's K
10.14	K belongs	13.28, 22.16	in K	13.29	feast in K	13.24, 13.44, 13.45, 13.47, 18.23 20.1, 22.2, 25.1	K is like this:
10.15	receive K	17.21	K is within you	16.16	good news about K	16.9	Keys of K
12.34	not far from K	18.29	the sake of K			19.12	the sake of K
14.25	in K					21.43	K taken away
						23.13	door to K
						24.14	good news about K

*Source: verses identified by Jeremias, 1971, p.31

This teaching is in some respects original, both for the terms and contents of the subject, and for its centrality as theme (Dalman, 1902; Jeremias, 1971). It is what Jesus taught, and it is Jesus' own teaching. What does it mean? Its meaning can be appreciated by considering its character and content.

Character

As Jesus' subject matter concerns a portending final event, it is eschatological in character; and as it concerns God, it can be viewed also as theological. Subjects of such a character were unexceptional in Jesus' milieu, although uncommon in our own. The particular subject of the Kingdom of God was familiar in Jewish ways of thinking and living at the time. But, treated as a conception, it is altogether alien to our ways of thinking about the world and the people in it, and it is ineffable in any given English word (Bultmann, 1934; Perrin, 1976). It is a subject not readily available to our categories of thought and language.

To appreciate the character of this subject, we may look to see how "Kingdom of God" was conceived in Jesus' milieu by contrast to how such a conception may be held in our own. This is already to treat it as a conception, and as an object of conceptual and linguistic analysis. We conceive of such a thing as "Kingdom of God" in spatial, abstract, static dimensions, and in propositional terms. By *negating* these we can come to perceive something of the Kingdom of God as Jesus taught it, although still seeing it in our terms, now contraries.

Kingdom of God is not a place but a function; not static and abstract but dynamic and concrete; not propositional but actional. It is activity: Kingdom is reigning, ruling; reign in action; that which king does as king; activity of ruling. It is not the idea or notion of the reigning but the action of it. Kingdom of God is "the reign of God in action," "the activity of God as king" (Jeremias, 1971; Perrin, 1976).

In just these terms, Jesus' aim of teaching this subject can also be perceived. It is possible to admire this Kingdom, or to fear it; to apprehend knowledge of it and to apply that knowledge, or not. But none of that is Jesus' aim. In complement to the subject matter, the aim of teaching it is not accomplished in spatial, abstract, static, or propositional forms. The aim is as actional in character as is the subject, and it too is constituted of an activity--something like the activity of *being* ruled by the ruling activity of God.

We have here made the Kingdom of God a subject of analysis and exposition, displaying it as an object of comprehension--distinctions to understand, points to grasp. That is not how it figured as the subject of Jesus' teaching. There, Kingdom of God is a point that grasps, a matter of which one is seized to act. For, that is how it was taken by the people to whom it was taught. Most of the people did not act in accordance with the subject as taught, but everyone understood it to be a matter of action.

Content

When people at the time saw and heard Jesus teach the coming Kingdom of God, they understood a content as well as character, the two constituting the meaning of his subject matter. What is the meaning?

It means first of all eschatological crisis. Things are at an end. The world is on the point of being transformed by the breaking-in of the Kingdom of God, as a visible cosmic irruption. This is the last, the final hour; God's ruling activity is beginning, and it is beginning now (Bultmann, 1934; Conzelmann, 1973). "This is what people will have heard in the call of Jesus: 'God is coming, he is standing at the door, indeed, he is already there'" (Jeremias, 1971, p.102). This is the crisis and event that calls for action. "Repent!"

If the present world is ending and a new one dawning, what is the Kingdom of God like? Jesus does not explain that; he depicts it in actions and parables (Aulen, 1976).

It is the case with the Kingdom of God, so Jesus teaches by action, *as it is the case with* feasting in fellowship with outcasts, elites, and marginal types together with casual and close friends and followers (Mk 2.15). It is the case as with naming outcasts and elites as disciples (Mt 10.3). It is the case as with healing the diseased and tormented (e.g., Mk 7.34). Satan's ruling is over, God's ruling activity begins. Jesus says: "The Kingdom of God is yours!" (L

6.20). His actions too proclaim that God's ruling is forgiveness in action; "God invites you to his festive meal" (Jeremias, 1971). It is a great reversal of everything now known, for, as was well known, not many could expect such an invitation, surely not those who actively failed to deserve one.

So also by parabolic speech does Jesus teach just that, depicting action amidst wholesale reversals. *It is the case with the Kingdom of God as it is the case with*:

> A man happens to find a treasure hidden in a field. He covers it up again, and is so happy that he goes and sells everything he has, and then goes back and buys that field. (Mt 13.44)

Also it is the case as with the good servants who are rewarded and the bad who are punished (eg., L 12.42-46), as with the bad servants who are rewarded (e.g., L 16.1-8). It is the case as with the Samaritan who acts like a good neighbor and the good men who do not (L 10.30-36). It is the case as with the rich man and a poor man who trade places, and a holy man and a sinful man who trade places (L 16.19-26, 18.10-14). It is the case as with the first-seated guests who get the worst places at table and the last-seated ones who get the best places, as it is with the invited guests who do not feast and the uninvited ones who do (Lk 14.7-11, 16-24). Also it is the case with the dutiful and the runaway sons: the runaway returns, the dead are alive, the lost are found, a feast is celebrated (L 15.11-32).

What do these depict? The Kingdom comes; the world reverses; action is joined (paraphrase of Crossan, 1973; the parabolic introductory, "It is the case with...as with," is from Jeremias, 1966). Parabolic actions and words give content to the subject: What? God's ruling activity; When? coming now; For whom? poor and rich, outcasts and elites--the distinctions no longer matter. Good and bad are reversed in antithetic parallelism, as with the first- and last-seated guests. That is not to deny the categories but to empty them of customary contents. What then is good, and what bad? The subject of Jesus' teaching runs only so far as to say that what is of God's ruling activity is first; what is not, is not. Make your choice and take your stand--now; for, the ruling of that which is not of God is over, and God's ruling is in process of beginning. Act!

Aim: "Repent"

Corresponding to the actional character of his subject matter, Jesus' aim of teaching it has the character of imperative action in the present. "Repent!" or "Turn away from your sins!" (Mk 1.15; Mt 4.17).

This kind of aim can be understood by reference to other aims whose kind it does *not* share:

The aim is not that learners acquire knowledge of the Kingdom of God, analyze its components, recite its definition and principles, deduce its consequences and implications.

The aim is not to appreciate or value the Kingdom of God, regard it with satisfaction or awe, admire or cherish it as an object of aesthetic attention and appeal.

The aim is not to apply the Kingdom of God, turning cognition and emotion to some good or useful purpose in life.

The aim is that learners act on it. The kind of action corresponds to the matter being taught. The action is urgent and immediate in face of the ending of the world, the ruling activity that is God's, and the coming of God's ruling now. As Jesus sees things, everything is at a knife-point; it is the last hour, a matter of life and death (Jeremias, 1971). Act now!

The radical and antithetic action in Jesus' parabolic conduct and speech betokens the *kind* of action aimed at. The parables call for a response on the spot; prompt and energetic decision, firm and resolute action (Crossan, 1973). Which individual actions are in view, among all those that may be prompt and decisive? As far as can be seen, particulars and specifics are not envisaged in Jesus' aim. The generic action aimed at seems to be one that puts God's ruling activity first--the activity of being ruled by God's ruling, and by none other. The rest follows, in details that seem of as little import as are the details in that present world now at an end, e.g., who is seated first and who last.

The action of "Repent" is generic--the turning away from sin and toward God. In the parable of the lost son, when the runaway begins to return, "he repented" (L15.17, per Jeremias 1971). The son who was lost and dead is now found and alive, and the feasting begins (v. 32). Jesus' action of feasting in fellowship with sinners tells that the Kingdom is forgiveness in action. His prayer is that the Kingdom come: "Forgive us our sins, as we are forgiving those who sin against us" (L 11.2, 4). To repent is to forgive and forsake sin in turning towards God's ruling activity. It is a new turn all around, a conversion of people in the convulsion of the world. Beyond that, Jesus does not aim.

Other Aims & Subjects

The Kingdom did not come, people did not repent. The question arises, whether Jesus had some other aim in view for teaching the Kingdom of God, or whether he also taught some other subjects with another aim. As far as can be known, he did not.

Aim describes intentionality joining teacher and learner activity in relation to subject matter. The generic aim of teaching is that the learner learn the subject being taught in a manner corresponding to that of the teaching act. In the case of instrumental subject matters, the aim is that the subject be learned in order that some further end be achieved, in relation to which that subject stands as means. No one knows the intents of Jesus. But his intentionality in teaching the Kingdom of God was, on the grounds cited, that those whom he taught should learn it; and, as his actions and words show him to have held nothing higher than God's ruling activity, he taught that subject with no further aim, there being no higher end that it could serve.

That people did not learn this subject as intended does not mean that Jesus did not teach it or that he did not aim that they learn it as intended. Rather, it signals the commonplace consideration that learners too hold aims and perform activities in relation to the subject matter being taught by the teacher with a given aim. Milieu is yet another factor implicated in the relations of teacher and learner, subject and aim.

Foremost among the subjects that Jesus did not teach is the matter of Jesus himself. He taught the Kingdom of God; his followers, after his death, taught "Jesus" (e.g., Acts 3.13). The corresponding purpose attributed to him, "becoming, being like Jesus" (Magness, 1975), informed not his but his followers' teaching activity.

Nor did Jesus teach principles of conduct or a way of life for individuals, communities, or society. He taught no system of values, no ethics at all. Having no conception of these, he did not teach morality, virtue, ends for conduct; social, political, or ethical programs; individualism, personality ideal, character-building; or world reformation (Bultmann, 1934). That which he did teach precludes these, for one cannot teach a system of ethics at the same time as the imminent end of everything in the world (Bultmann).

Modern criticisms of Jesus' ethical teachings (cited with disfavor by Preston, 1966) unwittingly demonstrate the positive point that he taught something other than ethics. The critics find in his teaching no truth, beauty, or justice; no teaching on political doctrine, war, capital punishment, gambling, or socialism; administration of law or distribution of goods; tyranny or self-determination; freedom or slavery; equality of income, sex, color, opportunity; and nothing about contraception. With some adjustment in perspective, all of these topics can be seen at work, some vividly, in Jesus' milieu. He taught nothing about them. He taught that the present world was coming to an end, and that a new age of God's ruling activity was dawning.

On that same account, furthermore, Jesus could not have held some ulterior or posterior aim in view for his teaching the Kingdom of God. He could aim at nothing higher and for nothing later. On the evidence of his own actions and words, observable by anyone and systematically assessed by historical, linguistic, literary, and rhetorical methods, Jesus was convinced that the world was coming to an end, and he expected it to end *soon*--in that present time, in that generation, in the lifetime of the people before him (Bornkamm, 1960; Bultmann, 1934; Jeremias, 1971; Kummel, 1961; Marshall, 1977; Wilder, 1971).

Among the aims that Jesus accordingly did not hold was to train for discipleship, to establish a church, and to begin a world-wide mission--e.g., "to train disciples to spread this faith and way of life in the world, . . . through them to transform other lives and regenerate human society" (Piper, 1931, p.34). These number among the developing aims of his followers' teaching activity, as they went about teaching "Jesus."

A multiplicity of other aims can be identified by observing what happened after Jesus' death and then retroactively attributing these events to Jesus as aims of his teaching activity, while proactively attributing to the events the character of results of his teaching activity. In that way his aims are seen to be accomplished, and his teaching successful. Neither these aims nor the success can be observed in his teaching activity, nor the subject matters and events on which they turn.

It remains possible to discover other aims of Jesus' teaching by fixing the notion at various levels of specificity, detailing aims, goals, purposes, ends, objectives, and outcomes. Education writers especially recognize the fluidity and capaciousness of these categories, and tend to value those statements which unambiguously and pointedly specify particulars of aim in relation to particulars of subject-matter, so as to guide particulars of teaching activity and the subsequent evaluation of its success in terms of objectives accomplished (e.g., Mager, 1962; Tyler, 1949). Those educators who have written on Jesus as a teacher tend to enumerate aims and objectives, as shown in Table 3. On the whole, these seem to miss the aim that Jesus held, whether for content, form, or number. They may well represent ends desired for teaching in some present circumstance, deduced from a view of what Jesus might have desired his followers to do, but they do not represent the aims of Jesus' teaching activity--imparting information about religion, solving life problems, forming character, training witnesses, dissolving race prejudice, etc. (Table 3).

It would be satisfying to express Jesus' aim in several and more specific formulations, but those in Table 3 do not seem to satisfy. More characteristic of Jesus is his single-mindedness, and more characteristic of his purpose is a generic rather than specific form and content.

Table 3. Educational Objectives Mistakenly Identified for Jesus

<u>Marquis, 1916</u>

1. impart religious knowledge
2. awaken thought about religion
3. induce decisions in behalf of religion
4. cultivate character
5. prepare for service

<u>Horne, 1920</u>

1. to do his Father's will & work
2. to be accepted as the Messiah
3. to win learners and to train them at witnesses of his
4. to substitute vital for formal religion
5. to fulfill the law in the new universal kingdom of social righteousness.
6. to show by example and to teach by precept the way of life
7. to quicken the faith & hope of men
8. to break the bonds of race prejudice
9. to destroy the works of darkness

<u>Squires, 1927</u>

1. <u>intellectual</u> - impart information about religion
2. <u>emotional</u> - develop appropriate emotional attitudes
3. <u>volitional</u> - apply religious truths to problems in conduct

<u>Richardson, 1931</u>

1. <u>individual</u> - restrain biological urges
2. <u>society</u> - improve environment

<u>Piper, 1931</u>

1. to lead disciples to trust & love God
2. to win their faith in him as Son of God
3. to teach the Christian way of life
4. to train disciples to spread this faith & way of life in the world

<u>Price, 1946</u>

1. form right ideals
2. fix strong convictions
3. convert to God
4. relate to others
5. meet life problems
6. train for service

The form and content of both Jesus' aim and subject matter remain to be fitted within or suited by categories established for educational aims and subjects. Writers in general education have classified these in numerous schemes. The most widely used current text on teaching (Joyce & Weil, 1992) displays two dozen models of teaching, grouped into four families; Jesus' activity of teaching fits none of these. The aim of his teaching is not described by any one of 17 objectives grouped into three missions--academic skills, personal capacity, social interaction--or by any of 10 outcomes of teaching. The most widely used taxonomy of educational objectives classifies these into a panoply of cognitive categories, affective categories, and psychomotor categories (Bloom, 1956; Krathwohl et al., 1964; Harrow, 1972), into none of which does Jesus' aim fall. The most eminent theorist of curriculum (Schwab, 1983) conceives that bodies of knowledge, skill, and taste may be taught and learned, as well as "propensity to act and react." Only this last covers Jesus' case, as a shadow.

Amidst this theoretical welter of things that can be taught and learned, Jesus' aim and subject matter find no easy place. That is not for their being non-academic or non-scholastic, for the majority of items so distinguished are non-academic and all are taught and learned in non-school settings as well. The universe being classified is education, not school, and the processes are teaching-learning, not didactic lecture and memorization of fact. This finding suggests that part of that universe remains to be classified to accommodate cases such as Jesus. It might otherwise suggest that Jesus is not a case of a teacher. But he was regarded as such by his contemporaries and he has been acclaimed as such in past and present times. Other teachers great and small, past and present, remain in a similar position beyond the ken of contemporary educational theory.

In contrast, theorists of religious education might comprehend the case of Jesus. The most rigorous and systematic of these devotes an entire long volume to the content of religious instruction (Lee, 1985). Content is conceived as an amalgam of 9 interactive elements in 5 groupings or dimensions: product/process, cognitive/affective, verbal/nonverbal, conscious/unconscious, and lifestyle. The Kingdom of God as Jesus taught it emerges fitfully to view as a conscious, nonverbal process, neither cognitive nor affective, and somewhat lifestylish. Another theorist devotes a chapter to the purpose of religious education (Groome, 1980). The overarching purpose is promoting a lived response to the Kingdom of God in Jesus Christ. Here is an aim and subject matter much like those that informed Jesus' teaching activity, with suitable accommodations made for present perspectives and purposes. And, much as with his case, they require endless shifting of categories and displays of distinctions before we can so much as come to grasp what is being taught and why.

Jesus did not teach that way. As he taught it, the subject and the aim were plainly enough matters of action now. "The Kingdom of God is near. Repent!"

Chapter 3

CIRCUMSTANCE OF TEACHING

Jesus taught in Palestine around the year 30 AD. Teaching always within Jewish milieux, he emerged in Galilee to the north and ended in the capital, Jerusalem, to the south. The circumstance of his teaching describes where and when and among whom he taught, here treated as milieu.

Milieu circumscribes a series of contexts, ranging from the most immediate and specific to the widest and most general, within which teaching and learning proceed. In the case of Jesus, as with other teachers, sense and significance accrue to the teaching-learning in virtue of the characteristics of the milieu, touching upon what and how he taught as also upon whom he taught--the subject, the aim, the activity of the teacher as well as the traits, activities, responses of the learners.

Not everything about first-century Palestine constitutes the milieu of Jesus' teaching, but only those aspects related to his teaching. Which aspects figured in the case of Jesus as a teacher, and conversely, how did he figure in the milieu?

Seen as widest circumstance, first-century Palestine accommodated not one but three milieux--a Hellenistic, a Roman, and a Judaic. Jesus may be situated within these by locating his teaching activity within the reign of Herod Antipas of Galilee (4BC-39AD), son of Herod the Great who died when Jesus was born (4BC); Tiberius Caesar of Rome (AD 14-37) and Pontius Pilatus the Roman prefect of Judea (26-36); and the high priest Joseph Caiaphas at Jerusalem (18-36). Although all three of these milieux impinged directly upon his teaching activity, Jesus moved through the greater part of this world as if it were not present. He taught exclusively within the Judaic milieu, scarcely adverting to the Hellenistic and the Roman, and teaching as if most of the Judaic milieu were irrelevant.

Graeco-Roman Milieux

The stuff and substance of the Hellenistic and Roman milieux together with their complicated and tense interactions with the Judaic, whether political, social, economic, philosophical, artistic, historical, religious or military, figure not at all in Jesus' teaching. There is nothing Graeco-Roman about what he taught, nor about the forms and language of his teaching, e.g., the parables; he did not teach to or about Greeks or Romans, nor in any of their cities--whether Tiberias, the largest, or Sepphoris, only four miles from his hometown of Nazareth (Conzelmann, 1973; Sherwin-White, 1963; Vermes, 1973). That stands by contrast to the long-time Hellenization of Palestine, most recently and intensively pursued by Herod the Great and continued apace by Herod Antipas; to the use of Greek as lingua franca in the area (Fitzmyer, 1979); and to the otherwise overriding fact of life unmistakable to anyone, that Palestine had been since a century past (63 BC) part of the Roman Empire, with Galilee a dependency and Judea a province (since 6AD), continually pacified by the veteran legions X Fretensis and XII Fulminata (among two others) together with Syrian auxiliaries as well as client armies, and garrisoned by six Sebastene regiments--not to mention the altogether larger Herodian army of Germans, Celts, Thracians, Galatians, Idumeans, and the non-Jewish like.

These milieux nonetheless impinged upon Jesus as a teacher, not the least by forming his learners and informing, by their construal, his subject, aim, and activity of teaching. The Hellenistic ruler of Galilee executed a prophet with whose person, message, and movement Jesus had been associated, John the Baptist; the Roman prefect of Judea executed Jesus. Jesus' conduct and message may have been construed as a kind of political activity counter to the established order. The Judaic milieu construed his teaching as a messianic movement, a restoration of the kingdom of Israel; and Graeco-Roman milieux construed accordingly.

The years just before, during, and after Jesus saw numerous revolts, uprisings, and insurrections terminating in the destruction and depopulation of the Jewish milieu and the edification upon the cleared debris of Jerusalem of a Graeco-Roman city, Hadrian's Aelia Capitolina. Some of these revolts preoccupied Galilee, the place of Jesus' origin and major teaching activity.

(The following events are a sample of those related by Flavius Josephus in Book II of *Wars of the Jews* and Books XVII-XX of *Antiquities of the Jews*; and by Jones, 1938.)

Just at the time that Jesus was born and the great Herod died (4 BC) a revolt by Judas "the Galileean," who was son of Hezekiah executed years before by Herod, was crushed by Publius Quinctilius Varus, governor of Syria, on his march to liberate Jerusalem from rebel occupation. There a Roman prefect and one legion were besieged after having suppressed a previous riot at the festival of Pentecost, by the device of burning down the Temple colonnades. That revolt had in turn been preceded by another one 50 days earlier at the great national festival of Passover, when Archelaus, son of Herod, had moved his entire army of 30,000, still mustered from his father's funeral procession, against rebels occupying the Temple, killing some 3,000 of them. Between this Passover and Pentecost, in Archelaus' absence, Varus had suppressed still other disorders and retired to Syria, leaving behind the one legion in Jerusalem now beset. Returning in force with two legions, auxiliaries, local levies, and client armies, Varus subdued Galilee and recaptured Jerusalem, crucifying 2,000 rebels and again leaving behind the one legion.

In the meantime revolts broke out elsewhere--"ten thousand other disorders" notes Josephus (*Antiquities*, XVII 10.4). Apart from Judas' revolt in Galilee, Perea rose under a Simon and Judea under Athronges, each of whom assumed a crown and raised armies; the first was defeated by Gratus, an Herodian infantry general, and the second, with four armies, was gradually reduced by Archelaus himself, and his generals Gratus and Ptolemy.

Galilee once again rose in revolt at the Roman census in 6 AD, again led by a Judas Galileean--"a teacher of a peculiar sect of his own" notes Josephus (*Wars* II 8.1). Judas formed together with the Pharisee Zadok the party of the "Zealots" to throw off foreign rule. Their revolt was crushed by another Roman governor of Syria, happening to be charged with the census, Publius Sulpicius Quirinius.

In Jesus' adult years, during the administration of the prefect Pontius Pilatus (26-37), a series of violent acts and reactions marked both sides, notable even at that time for their bloodiness and ruthlessness (Schalit, 1969;

Vermes, 1973). One notorious event was referred to as Pilate's massacre of Galileeans in the act of worship, mingling their blood with the blood of their sacrifices, and so on. The occasion was a riot in the Temple at some festival, over Pilate's use of Temple funds to build aqueducts.

Revolts continued apace after Jesus' death, forming to everyone's eye one continuous theme of the milieu, under each of the successive Roman prefects. One event for each will be noted. Around the year 45, a prophet named Theudas brought to the Jordan River for its promised cleavage at his wave, a large following promptly dispersed by the cavalry of Cuspius Fadus (44-46); Theudas was executed and his head posted in Jerusalem as a warning to other prophets. In the next two years a revolt was raised by the Galileean brothers James and Simon, sons of Judas the Galileean who had revolted after Herod's death; Tiberius Julius Alexander (46-48) handled their affair by crucifying them. A few years later during a Passover riot, thousands perished, trampled in the panic of Ventidius Cumanus' (48-52) attack. Next a prophet from Egypt gathered his 30,000 followers outside Jerusalem to demonstrate before their eyes the collapse of its walls at his command, only to disappear before the armed command of Marcus Antonius Felix (52-60); the prophet escaped, and one of Felix' commanders wondered whether his new prisoner Paul of Tarsus were not that revolutionary figure (Acts 21.38). Yet another prophet subsequently arose with a formidable following to be beaten down by the next prefect, Porcius Festus (60-62). Under the next-to-last, Clodius Albinus (62-64), Jesus' own brother James was stoned to death. With the final prefect, Gessius Florus, Josephus dates the start of the great Jewish rebellion against Rome, ending in the obliteration of the Jewish milieux.

While such events preoccupied populations and authorities and form the stuff of any history written of the time, Jesus' teaching ignored them altogether. Yet they happened around him just as around everyone else, and he was aware of contemporary instances such as Herod's beheading of the messianic Baptist (Mt 14.12) and Pilate's massacre of Galileeans at worship (L 13.1). His indifference to them notwithstanding, these events form part of the milieu of his teaching and as such they saw assigned to it an essential character that was neither of its essence nor of its accidents as he taught it. For it was on grounds of these kinds that he was arrested and executed, certainly as a criminal and perhaps as a political rebel or agitator.

The specifics are not known. It is known that Roman officials crucified Jesus in Jerusalem during the Jewish national festival of Passover. Riots and insurrections there and then were anticipated on all sides; on that account the prefect Pontius Pilatus would leave his seat at Caesarea Philippi and betake himself to Jerusalem for the occasion, along with reinforcements for the garrison. Into this city came Jesus with some followers. There he taught in the Temple. In the Temple he also did something violent (Mk 11.15-16) that may have constituted or provoked an attempted seizure of it, a demonstration, a melee, a clamor, for which or during which he may have been arrested.

By all accounts, Jesus' going to and teaching in Jerusalem appears to have been a decisive move, perhaps to confront the Judaic milieu to a decision in its very center of religious (and national, etc.) existence and authority. "The Kingdom of God is near! Repent!" The populace could have construed this teaching as a politico-religious event; that construction, together with its popular implications at that specific time and place, may have been cause enough for the official milieu to act or to react decisively against Jesus. These together with the violence in the Temple, or that violence alone, may have led to his arrest. To outsiders common or elite--as indeed to his followers and closer disciples--the teaching was recognizably political; his appearance in Jerusalem was interpretable as an attack on the foundations of religion--which indeed his teaching conduct and content were--and also of the nation; and the Temple fierceness looks much like an insurrection (Bultmann, 1934; Conzelmann, 1973; Fuchs, 1964).

On the other hand, the Temple affair may have been a small one, an act by Jesus alone. None of his followers is depicted or implicated in the action, no disciples are arrested with him, none hunted down and executed--not then, not later. The scene as we have it shows no officious reaction at all, not to mention that impressively speedy and decisive riposte afforded to all known disturbances before, after, and during Jesus' lifetime (Catchpole, 1984).

Furthermore, not only do we not see Jesus arrested on the spot, we see no one about who could arrest him: he is the lone actor, in a circumstance absent the usual police, guards, troops and those everyday Jewish, Herodian, and Roman superstructures which they so customarily and effectively served and protected. Quite apart from the Jewish Temple guard and the usual police and security agents all about, the Roman authorities made a point of covering the Temple as well as other parts of the city. Josephus has to make special mention of this in order to account for a Passover riot in the Temple that was occasioned by a Roman soldier's obscene exhibition to the crowd: "a Roman cohort stood over the cloisters of the temple (for they always were armed and kept guard at the festivals, to prevent any innovation which the multitude thus gathered together might make)" [*Wars* II 12.1]. Jesus' act makes it appear as if the milieux were not present--and not only as not depicted. The unmistakable directness and violence of Jesus' action shows it to have been undertaken and executed precisely as if the milieu were indeed not there to be counted. Here again is the character of action taken in the very face of the milieu without taking any notice of it.

In any event, the one certainty is that the Roman milieu, so entirely ignored by his teaching, here came conclusively to touch upon it, putting Jesus to an end.

Judaic Milieu

It was within Jewish milieux that Jesus taught. He himself was a Jew, and he taught Jews; the content of his teaching, the forms and language, illustrations, appeals, and referents were all Jewish. The Judaic milieu was in essence a religious entity and Jesus was a Jewish religious teacher.

All other facets of life and individual preoccupations notwithstanding, this milieu was informed by religion. Religion was the organizing theme around which circled otherwise separable motifs of nation, state, society, politics, economics, history, literature, and the rest. These are now commonly conceived as slices or departments of life, each with a claim as a distinctive milieu by itself, permissibly related to the others but standing apart from them. The world of first-century Jewish Palestine subsumed all of these within the Judaic milieu defined by religion. That was the official definition.

Insofar as the milieu defined itself and represented this definition to itself in publicly observable forms, the central facts of life were religious. The milieu was preoccupied with themes of law and eschatology, election and salvation. The Jews had been chosen by God to be his people. They governed themselves in expectation of a time when God's kingship should manifest itself in a cosmic gathering of his people unto himself, elevating them above all others on earth. It was within this sort of milieu that Jesus taught. And it is these kinds of themes and preoccupations that informed his teaching. But on every count he taught that the case was otherwise than commonly assumed to be.

The Kingdom of God, according to Jesus, was becoming a reality in the present moment, about to break into the cosmos. Nothing about it, so he taught by doing and saying nothing about that, concerns a terrestrial establishment of the Jewish nation-state. To the contrary, the entire present world is at an end. God's ruling activity is beginning. Membership in a chosen people and individual observance of law guarantee nothing; repenting is the decisive activity as God's ruling activity comes in. Teachings such as these, and the actions whereby Jesus taught them, manifestly reversed the present scheme of things, making the whole of it of no concern.

The milieu construed this teaching according to the proprieties. If, for example, the elect and the law-abiding are not for that fact the elite and the saved, and if the outcasts and the sinners are not for that fact excluded and damned--then this is a repugnant new teaching counter to all right sensibilities of religion, nation, law, and the rest; or it is a welcome new teaching penetrating to the heart of all things right and Jewish. On neither side was the matter academic. For Jesus, discussion of either side of it was academic, for the world was at an end and action was joined. In all respects Jesus' teaching locates at the very center of the milieu.

At a next narrower circle of this milieu there formed various groupings, all necessarily defined by religious characteristics. The religious characteristics in turn necessarily defined, by entailment, a social character, a political character, and so forth. The most salient official groupings were the priests, the scribes, and the Pharisees (as described by Jeremias, 1971).

Priests formed a group charged with carrying on public worship in Jerusalem. They achieved priesthood not by theological study but by consecration in virtue of heredity, membership in a priestly family. Most were found scattered about the area; in Jerusalem there was found a rich priestly nobility.

Scribes came to their position from all levels of society, through special training and ordination as theologians. They functioned as (religious) teachers and judges, making authoritative decisions on matter of religious and penal law.

Pharisees formed a small, lay group--whose leaders were Scribes--chiefly of merchants and craftsmen who gathered in conventicles and assumed the defining duties of observing the tithe and regulations for ritual purity or cleanliness. They were notable for their charity, prayer, and fasting, and they referred to themselves as the pious, the righteous, the God-fearing, and especially "the separated ones" (whence, "pharisee")--i.e., that group which above all would be found by God to be gathered into his kingdom when it came.

A mix of these groupings yielded the *Sadducees*, conservative defenders of the written law against oral innovators and even oral traditionalists. A privileged class by birth, they counted property owners, landed nobility, chief priests and other wealthy types, from which were drawn the occupants of the highest offices in the Jewish government--the high priest and his advisors, the majority of the Supreme Council, the commanders of the Temple guard, the treasurers and other notable functionaries. Conservative toward cult, law, and other national institutions, Sadducees showed themselves accommodating of foreign powers--Rome, Herod--for their class interests not surprisingly favored peace and quiet on all sides (Schalit, 1971; Winter, 1971).

A recombination of 71 individuals from these mixed groupings formed the specific body of the *Supreme Council*, or Sanhedrin. It numbered 8-10 chief priests, specifically the high priest and the priest in charge of the Temple, together with a few priests from the nobility--secular aristocrats all--and some financial experts. Other members were Elders, patrician landowners often residing beyond Jerusalem (thus rarely in attendance), and Scribes, of whom the majority were Sadducees and the minority Pharisees. The Council chairman, ex-officio, was the high priest, a personage whose individual identity was determined not without reference to the opinion of the Roman prefect, who, also ex officio, denominated him (Reicke, 1971). In Jesus' time, the high priest was Caiaphas.

Another group of separated ones were the *Essenes*, ascetics who withdrew from the Temple worship into the wilderness as an eschatological community. *Zealots* committed themselves to freeing the Jewish nation of foreign dominance and to restoring a kingdom of Israel. They were not known for patient pursuit of political opposition but for raiding parties of "resistance fighters." A number of other messianic movements appeared from time to time, including that of *John the Baptist* from which Jesus emerged.

These are the somewhat official and notable groupings forming the smaller milieux within which Jesus taught, along with multiple other groups that can be identified less officially and clearly. The latter would include uncollected classes of individuals who were called outcasts, who were collaborators with Roman occupation, who were notorious sinners against the law, who were religiously ignorant, who were poor, who were rich, who were male, who were female, and so forth. Jesus moved among all of these and taught individuals from among all of them. Together they are the milieux that form the Judaic milieu of Jesus' teaching activity.

At its most narrow and most specific, the milieu of Jesus' teaching circumscribes the immediate place and time of a given teaching activity. This milieu is not defined by characteristics of place or time, such as might be designated or appointed for teaching activity. Rather it is characteristic of Jesus that he taught more or less everywhere and anytime.

Jesus did indeed sit and receive people who came to be taught. He also went out and about teaching people as he found them. He did sit and teach in synagogues and he stood and taught in the Temple. He also taught in his home and in other homes, at table, out in the country, in fields, by the seashore, in a boat, and along the road. For a time he centered his teaching activity around his own town of Capernaum, north in Galilee, and for a time in the great city of Jerusalem, south in Judea; and he also taught in a dozen other named towns around and between these, as well as in unnamed towns and villages identified by numerous regional locations.

Not all of these towns and villages are rightly pictured as rustic habitations of dusty insignificance apart from their gospel mention, for they were well enough known in their own time and for their own role in the milieu. Quite apart from the overriding case of Jerusalem there is, for example, Capernaum, where Jesus maintained a home for a time. But it was also a military station and customs post on the trade route from Damascus, seat of the Roman governor among other things, to Caesarea, a coastal port founded by Herod, graced by the residence of the Roman procurator, and garrisoned by several cohorts. Jericho too was a trading city.

A sample of towns and places of Jesus' teaching activity, as specified in Mark's gospel, is given in Table 4.

These specifications serve to localize the immediate milieu of Jesus' teaching activity and to characterize, among other aspects, his use of milieu. It is as if any situation or context might serve for the teaching act, and every one turned to the occasion. It follows as well that the learners were anybody and everyone (Jewish).

Salience of Jesus

Just as the milieu figured in Jesus' teaching, so also Jesus figured in the milieu. On several counts Jesus can be seen to stand out against the milieu but on no account can he be seen as an outstanding figure within it. Those who took notice of him could perceive several original characteristics of his teaching, yet he was little enough noticed.

Among Jesus' many original characteristics as a teacher, viewed always in light of his milieu, are those that range through the categories of subject and aim, conduct and language, learner and milieu. For instance of the latter, his teaching was antithetical to contemporary religiosity and religious thinking, and he pursued teaching activity outside of customary places and times and people. Both his conduct and his language as a teacher were original in substance and form, the whole of it recognizably self-authoritative by contrast to customary modes of teaching (e.g., interpretation of text, citation of authorities). These features were strikingly marked by his characteristic and notable manner of saying "You have heard it said..., but I say to you..." or "Amen, I say to you..." rather than "Thus saith the Prophets/Lord/Law, amen." The subject and aim of

Table 4. The Immediate Milieu of Jesus' Teaching

Places			Towns & Villages			Regions		
synagogue	Mk	1.21	Nazareth	Mk	1.9	Galilee	Mk	1.39
seashore		2.13	Capernaum		1.21	Gerasa		5.1
boat		4.1-2	Chorazin	Lk	10.13	Tyre		7.24
country		1.45	Nain		7.11	Sidon		7.31
road		10.17	Bethsaida	Mk	6.45	Decapolis		7.31
home		2.1-2	Gennesaret		6.43	Caesarea Philippi		8.27
fields		2.23ff	Jericho		10.46	Dalmanutha		8.10
others' homes		14.3	Bethpage		11.1	TransJordan		10.1
Temple		12.35,41	Bethany		11.1	Judea		10.1
Mt. of Olives		13.3	Gethsemane		14.32			
			Jerusalem		11.27			

his teaching were original both for content and for expression: "The Kingdom of God is near! Repent now!"

Yet none of that is to suggest that Jesus' teaching figured prominently in the milieu. The extent to which it loomed is not known but appears to have been limited if not minimal. He taught here and there for not much more than one year in all. His teaching was well enough received in some milieux and repugned in others, with equal intensity of reaction. On no account does he appear as a well-known, "popular" or leading figure in the milieu.

No history of first-century Palestine can be written today without mentioning Jesus; and some accounts will mention the Palestine of that day only by reference to him. But at that time histories and other accounts of Palestine and things Judaic--not to mention the wider world--were in fact composed with no mention or reference whatsoever to Jesus, as were those by Josephus (*Jewish Wars*, *Jewish Antiquities*). Josephus mentions everything but. The accounts specify all manner of local messiahs and insurrectionaries, provincial uprisings and disturbances, with dates, names, places, numbers and casualties, causes and effects, beginnings and endings--and without a word about Jesus, his teaching, his followers. No contemporary chronicles or documents mention Jesus. (The gospels are neither contemporary nor documentary.) In later times and other places, teaching about Jesus caused more than a stir; the teaching of Jesus in his milieu did not. His teaching seems not to have made so much a stir as John the Baptist's had (Jones, 1938).

Both were executed, Jesus for a cause perhaps not of his own teaching or perhaps before his teaching showed itself to cause more of a stir--an effect in any event irrelevant to the teaching as he conducted it.

Whatever the case may have been, it is not known to be that Jesus' teaching figured prominently in the milieu. Just as Jesus seems to have moved through the milieu teaching as if it were not actually present--the Hellenistic, the Roman, the Judaic circles and preoccupations--so too the milieu proceeded on the whole as if Jesus were not actually teaching within it. For him the milieu took but one sharp moment of conclusive notice, itself noted only by his friends.

The Kingdom did not come, people did not repent, and things remained as before. When Jesus' friends began to teach, things began to happen and long notice was taken throughout the Hellenistic, Roman, and Judaic milieux. It was their teaching about him rather than his teaching about the Kingdom that figured prominently in the milieu.

Chapter 4

CORRESPONDENTS OF TEACHING

As he went out and about Jewish milieux, Jesus taught people of all kinds (all of them Jews). The dispositions that they brought to the situation, their own activity in the teaching-learning process, and their response to the teaching serve to characterize them as either opponents or adherents of Jesus. But all of them are in the first place the correspondents of his teaching: they are the people whom Jesus taught. What they learned is another matter.

People Taught by Jesus

Just as Jesus went about teaching everywhere and anytime, so he taught everyone there and then, in all manner of contexts and so to all kinds of people. The character of his message as well as the urgency with which he taught it also show that he taught anyone at hand in any circumstance. His parabolic actions and speech further make it plain that distinctions held most important at the time among people and between groups meant nothing either way: all were called to respond to the coming reign of God; all were correspondents of his teaching. The character of his correspondents varied accordingly, and indiscriminately.

Kinds of correspondents

A sample of correspondents appears in Table 5. They are arranged in groupings, with one example given for each group. These are the *kinds* of people that Jesus taught.

Table 5. Kinds of People Taught by Jesus

STATUS		LOCALE		COLLECTIVITY	
Elites					
Pharisees	Lk 7.36	Urban	Mk 12.34	Individuals	Mk 14.3
Scribes	Mk 12.28	Rural	Mk 6.6	Groups	Mk 3.32
Sadducees	Mk 12.18			Congregations	Mk 1.21
Priests	Mk 11.27			Crowds	Mk 2.13
Elders	Lk 7.3-4				
Synagogue officials	Mk 5.22				
Council members	Mk 15.43				
Baptist disciples	Lk 7.20				
Zealots	Mk 3.18				
Rich	Mk 10.22				
Marginals					
Poor	Lk 6.20				
Women	Lk 10.39				
Ill - diseased	Mk 1.40				
disabled	Mk 2.5				
possessed	Mk 5.2				
Outcasts					
Sinners	Lk 7.37				
Tax-collectors	Mk 2.15				

In the Judaic milieu of first-century Palestine, the most important kind of grouping to which people could belong was defined by religious character. Right religious character, in a milieu itself defined by religion, brought with it by entailment a mix of social, political, and economic attributes which together established elite status. Wrong character established the outcasts, and indifferent character the marginals. People of all of these kinds were taught by Jesus (Table 5).

Of the *elites*, Jesus most frequently taught the right-living, God-fearing Pharisees. He characteristically also taught members of the religious officialdom, particularly scribes and synagogue officials but also Sadducees, priests, elders. And he taught those who belonged to ascetic, messianic, religious-nationalist movements such as those of the Zealots and John the Baptist. In view of his teaching, Jesus had a great deal to do with elites and much to say to them, as also they to him. He not only found himself teaching them but also found among them followers and disciples.

What was more remarkable at the time is that Jesus taught *marginal types* such as women and ignorant "people of the land". And most remarkable of all, he taught *outcasts* such as tax-collectors and sinners. He was notorious for associating with these rightly despised people, even eating and drinking with them as their guest and host at festive meals. Further, Jesus taught--moreover, he touched--people to shun for dreaded disease, ritual uncleanliness, and demonic torment. Among all of these types too Jesus found followers and disciples.

On other counts of character, Jesus taught people who lived in the great center of Jerusalem and in some lesser cities or urban territories of Palestine, as well as people from towns, villages, and farms. So also he taught the rich and poor, the educated and unschooled. He taught individuals and also people collected in groups, congregations, and crowds as he went about outdoors and in, at home and synagogue, alongside sea, field, hill, and road.

Just as Jesus did not teach only at times and places appointed for teaching, so neither did he teach only those people designated as recipients of teaching in situations designated for teaching and learning. It is not characteristic of him to have taught people designated as pupils or students or disciples. It is not characteristic of those whom he taught to have forgathered about him or to have sat before him in rooms, halls, synagogues, porticoes and courts, there to receive his instruction. What is characteristic is that he taught non-designated learners in non-designated learning situations. The people whom Jesus taught are of all kinds.

Kinds of responses

In their character as learner in relation to Jesus as teacher, the diverse correspondents serve as complement to him in the teaching situation--by bringing to it, as he did, purposes, understandings, dispositions and other traits and dynamics; by engaging, as he did, in activity of teaching-learning; by figuring, as he did, within milieux circumscribing and construing teacher and learner as they interacted over subject matter in circumstance. In complement to asking what the teacher was like and how he taught, one asks what these people were like whom Jesus taught, and what they did as they acted with him. The eventual answer will describe the learning that resulted. All of the people whom Jesus taught learned. The eventual question will be, *Who learned what*? (see chapter 7 herein)

Only a very few of the learners are known as individuals, and little enough about them is known. The individuals can be characterized by the device of inferring from their engagement in teaching-learning some personality type to attribute to them. In this way specified individuals have been typed as the perplexed, frivolous, repentant, despised, inquiring, sorrowful, sanguine, choleric, despondent, lethargic, unsympathetic, hostile, cynical, and self-righteous (Griffith-Jones, 1902). Far too little--next to nothing--is seen of the individuals to justify such ascriptions, not the less to typify any one by this or that single personality trait. In any event, personality played no role in the textual sources and was unknown in the milieu; people were known by status, grouping, and especially by action. In the particular case of Jesus' teaching, it was action that informed his subject matter and aim, it was by actions that he taught, and above all it was by action that his learners were defined and known. All of the people whom Jesus taught can be characterized, inasmuch as correspondents of his teaching, as either positively or negatively disposed, active, and responsive. They are not either positive or not, they are either positive or negative.

The grounds for this polar characterization are not theoretical but derive from the pragmatics of the case. People are seen to be, act, and respond to Jesus' teaching either negatively or positively. The case appears to merit either one but only one or the other. Jesus is seen to be, act, and respond in just that same way. He is pressing and insistent, affrontively demanding and immediate, single-mindedly uncompromising about the absolute claim that God's ruling activity makes upon this person here and now. Above all, Jesus is antithetical. His actions and words are always a case of this versus that, the one not negating but *reversing* the other. As for the people he taught, Jesus asserts in characteristically antithetical form: "Anyone who is not for me is against me" (Mt 12.30). All the correspondents of Jesus' teaching are on these grounds either opponents or adherents.

Opponents of Jesus

These are the people who receive Jesus' teaching with "a storm of indignation," taking it as "a slap in the face to all the religious feelings of the time" (Jeremias, 1971, p.118). The individuals among them are not known. Opponents are known by groupings, particularly of religious character.

Opponent groups

Of the religious groups, the *Pharisees* had most frequently to do with Jesus, and they characteristically rejected his teaching. They had good reason for doing so. For, by his actions and words Jesus taught that the religious practices and beliefs typified by Pharisaism were far from the heart of that very Kingdom of God to which the Pharisees above all people aspired and into which they saw themselves apart from all others being gathered by God's favorable finding of them. Jesus taught to the very contrary. It was not on these accounts of practice and belief that Pharisees would find themselves so much as included in the Kingdom, while even notorious sinners and despised outcasts would not on these contrary accounts be excluded. "I tell you," he declared -- to their face -- "the tax collectors and the prostitutes are going into the Kingdom of God ahead of you" (Mt 21.31).

This surely was a new teaching, and at very least a scandalous and offensive one. It was not mere negation but the very antithesis of all things known and true--as if the good were bad and the bad good! And it was antithetical to those right religious sensibilities possessed by Pharisees above all others, by definition--it was *they* who were the pious, the righteous, the separated, God-fearing ones. In actions and words, Jesus' teaching called this definition into question by dismissing its grounds in religious behavior and conviction. Pharisees in turn questioned Jesus' teaching, especially his conduct (Mk 2.24); and they characteristically rejected it, on equally foursquare religious grounds.

People in other religious groups too opposed Jesus' teaching. These included the teachers, judges, and defenders of the law called *Scribes* (Mk 2.6) and *Sadducees* (12.18), some of whom were also leading Pharisees; as well as *elders* (11.27), *priests* (11.18) and officials of *synagogues* (Lk 13.14). As was customary, they would question a teacher, ascertain his authority, test his knowledge, probe his conduct, and generally engage him in exchanges over points of law, tradition, and the rest. As a group, these people are seen to have found Jesus a worthy interlocutor but wanting in right conduct and conviction.

Finally, people from a non-religious and non-Jewish group opposed Jesus' teaching, the party of the *Herodians* (Mk 12.13). The opposition was likely political in the main.

Herod the Great had adroitly come to terms with vast powers right and left, such as Rome and Parthia, energetically maintaining personal rule in the area as well as a phenomenal pursuit of building and Hellenization. His program also included regular and markedly incisive suppressions of insurrection and disorder. These continued apace during the rule of Herod's sons over parts of the area in Jesus' lifetime. Archelaus (4BC-6AD) suppressed an uprising in Jerusalem, and Herod Antipas executed the leader of a messianic movement, John the Baptist (28 AD). Jesus had been associated with that movement, lived through Herod's execution of its leader, and continued to have relations with its followers, some of whom attached themselves to him. Certainly to political eyes Jesus looked to be of the same stripe, and he may have been pressed to leave the Galilee of Herod Antipas (Lk 13.31).

Continuing in the same vein, Herod Agrippa I executed James (Acts 12.1-2), one of Jesus' closest adherents, some years after (42 AD) Jesus had been executed in Jerusalem by the Romans; while in those same years, as if in similar vein, Roman authorities suppressed at least two outbreaks by Galileeans, one in Jerusalem itself (49), the other led by Jacob and Simon (46-48), sons of that Judas "the Galileean" who had led at least two revolts in the early years of Jesus' life (4BC, 6AD), forming for such purpose the party of Zealots to which at least one of Jesus' closest adherents was known by name to belong, Simon "the Zealot" (Mk 3.18). These too were seen as messianic movements, like John's and Jesus' (Bultmann, 1934). They form a characteristic of the Jewish and particularly Galileean scene at the time (Shalit, 1969; Vermes, 1973). As such they must also in some regard have informed Jesus' correspondents in the milieu of teaching and learning.

Doubtless some of the opposition to Jesus from religious officials, who like the Herods had also come to terms with maintaining things and themselves in their present status, and some of the opposition from non-official Jewish correspondents too, was informed by political and national concerns.

Opponent responses

Pharisees, Scribes and these others are seen in typical scenes to question and to criticize Jesus' teaching, and also to warn and to threaten him on these accounts. The settings reflect the disputations, controversies and conflicts which Jesus had characteristically to engage in, revealing the typical responses of opponents as also Jesus' typical riposte in defense of his conduct and attitudes (Bultmann, 1968; Hultgren, 1979). His characteristic move was to reply in form of a counter-question, to the effect of regaining control of the exchange and then conclusively pronouncing on the opponent's enforced reply or silence (Dillon, 1981b).

Pharisees and the rest challenge his authority (Mk 6.2-3, 11.27-30), his interpretation of law (12.14-17), his conduct and attitudes toward the law--observance of the Sabbath (Mk 2.23-28; Lk 13.10-16), fasting (Mk 2.18-20), and ritual purity (7.2-8). They accuse him of exorcising by the power of the very devil himself (Mk 3.22-30), and of blaspheming against God himself by forgiving sinners (Mk 2.1-12; Lk 7.48-50). In vivid taunts, they score his lack of asceticism, his eating and drinking (Mt 11.19; Lk 15.2), and they especially excoriate him for associating with sinners and outcasts (Mk 2.15-17; Lk 7.39; Mt 11.19). Over each of these points they engage with Jesus, and he with them. As a group they did not learn what he was teaching them of these matters.

Other collectivities also rejected Jesus' teaching. These include congregations in synagogues where he taught (Mk 6.2-3); towns where he taught--and lived--Nazareth, Capernaum, Chorazin, Bethsaida (Lk 10.13-15); regions and provinces where he taught--Gerasa (Mk 5.17), and Galilee as a whole.

Into the face of all of these Jesus hurled god-awful curses and insults in the most vituperative language imaginable--against whole towns (Lk 10.13-15), against Herodians (Lk 13.32), against synagogue officials (Lk 13.15) and priests (Mk 11.17), most particularly against Scribes and Pharisees (Mt 21.1-33), and generally against anyone who was not for him (Mt 12.30). Jesus gave no middle ground. All the remaining correspondents had therefore to be, on his terms, adherents of Jesus.

Adherents of Jesus

Pharisees also accepted Jesus' teaching, as did members of other elite groups. So also did people on the fringe of society, in the outcasts, and ordinary people in between. These adherents did not form a group, such as the Pharisees did, identified by some characteristic or feature; rather they represent a category or class of uncollected and unassembled people who were receptive to Jesus' teaching. Just as those who figured as Jesus' opponents rejected his teaching on several grounds, not uniformly religious ones, so also did his adherents accept it on various counts, in various respects, to various degrees.

The adherents, followers, companions, disciples and the like are, as far as they are known, assembled for convenient reference in Table 6. These include examples of all possible instances detectable by "audience criticism" of the gospel texts as together forming the "disciple 'crowd'" (Baird, 1969).

Outside of Table 6 they form no whole save for their character as people receptive to Jesus' teaching.

Groupings of adherents

The people receptive to Jesus can be sorted into a number of non-exclusive classes, grouped by status and gender, by individuality and collectivity, by named and unnamed identity (Table 6). These form conceptual groupings but not physical assemblages.

Among the elites as well as the outcasts were found adherents and not alone opponents. Leading *Pharisees* such as Simon invited Jesus to their homes to share in table fellowship, to discourse with him, and to learn from his parables and actions (Lk 7.36, 11.37, 14.1). In their exchanges with him, *Scribes* too responded positively and became followers of Jesus (Mk 12.32, Mt 8.19), and Jesus spoke of Scribes entering the Kingdom (Mk 12.34; Mt 13.52). *Elders* too showed themselves receptive (Lk 7.3), as did *synagogue officials* like Jairus (Mk 5.22-23) and *Council members* like Joseph, a Pharisee from Arimathea (Mk 15.40). Members of *John the Baptist's* movement accepted him (Mk 7.20; Lk 7.29), and some like the brothers Simon and Andrew were counted among his closer disciples (Jn 1.35), along with Simon, a member of the *Zealots* party (Mk 3.18). Even *Herodians* became disciples, such as Joanna the wife of Chuza, who was an officer in Herod's court (Luke 8.3); or showed like the Herodian officer a receptivity to Jesus (Lk 7.2, 9).

Adherents in marginal groups were found among women and the sick who turned to follow Jesus and to count as disciples. Adherents among the *sick* included the Samaritan leper (Lk 17. 19), the blind Bartimaeus (Mk 10.52), the ritually unclean woman who suffered from hemorrhaging (Mk 5.34), the demented Gerasene (Mk 5.18), and the tormented Mary Magdalene (Mk 15.40). Adherents among *women* were counted in the followers of Jesus in Galilee and in Jerusalem (Mk 15.40-41; Lk 23.27), and in the group of followers hiding after Jesus' execution (Lk 24.22). As for individuals, a woman praised Jesus from the crowd (Lk 11.27), a Mary sat at his feet listening to his teaching while he was guest in her home, and other named followers were Joanna, Martha, Mary Magdalene, Mary the mother of James and Joseph, Salome, and Susanna (see Table 6).

Adherents were also found among the outcasts, such as *sinners* (Lk 7.37) and other immoral and despised lowlife, most especially *tax-collectors* (Mk 2.15; Lk 7.29, 15.1). Three tax-collectors are known by name as disciples of Jesus: Levi (Mk 2.14), Matthew (Mt 10.3), and Zacchaeus (Lk 19.8).

A number of *unnamed individuals* appear as Jesus' adherents (e.g., Lk 9.57), as also do *collections of people* in groups sitting about Jesus in a house or crowding about him here and there outdoors (Table 6). The number of adherents, to be distinguished from the size of crowds before him, is unknown. There are "a large number of disciples" accompanying Jesus (Lk 6.17, 19.37); there are the "the 70" (Lk 10.1); there are "120" (Acts 1.15) and "500" (I Cor 15.6) gathering days after Jesus' death. These numbers are symbolic of something other than the count of disciples, while their number is never counted.

Lastly there is the group of disciples fixed soon after Jesus' death as *The Twelve*. All of them are named, counted and listed together as The Twelve, called apostles as well as disciples (see Table 6). Their number too is symbolic of something else (the twelve tribes of Israel), suggesting that the most appropriate dozen of some number of individuals were fitted into the twelve rather than twelve being the number to fit the most appropriate individuals.

Three of The Twelve are depicted as Jesus' most constant intimates. They are Simon, son of Jonas, so named in Hebrew, also called by the Aramaic Cephas and traditionally by the Greek, Peter; and the two sons of Zebedee, James and John, nicknamed "Boanerges" or sons of thunder. These three came from Capernaum, where Jesus lived and taught; they were or had been fishermen, and followers of John the Baptist. The other nine are Andrew, Simon's brother; Philip, Bartholomew, and Thomas; Matthew, a tax-collector, and Simon, a Zealot or patriot; James son of Alphaeus and Thaddeus son of James; and Judas from Kerioth, invariably listed last and identified as having betrayed Jesus (e.g., Mk 3.19).

Little is known or even seen of most of these individuals, especially during Jesus' lifetime--which also is the case with his other disciples. The group that these twelve are made to form is in character similar to that of the whole group of disciples in that it, no more than the other, was not an

Table 6. Adherents of Jesus

Grouping or Types*	Named Individuals		"THE TWELVE"** Name	Other Name	Origin
1. Those with "The Twelve" disciples - Mk 4.10	Bartimaeus	Mk 10.52	Peter & Andrew	Simon, Cephas	sons of John at Capernaum; fishermen; followers of John the Baptist
	Cleophas	Lk 24.18			
2. Those following Jesus in a crowd- Lk 7.11	Jairus	Mk 5.22-23	James & John	"Boanerges" (sons of rage or thunder)	sons of Zebedee and (?) Salome at Capernaum; fishermen, (?) partners of Peter & Andrew; (?) followers of John the Baptist
	Joanna	Lk 8.3			
3. Certain ones who almost followed Jesus "wherever you go" Lk 9.57	Joseph-Barsabbas	Acts 1.23			
	Joseph of Arimathea	Mk 15.43	Philip		not the Philip/s in Acts 6.5, 8.26, 21.8
4. Certain women "of our company" - Lk 24.22	Levi	Mk 2.14			
	Martha	Lk 10.38	Bartholomew	(?Nathaniel)	(?) son of Tolmay
5. Certain godly people - Mk 12.34	Mary, Martha's sister	Lk 10.39	Thomas	"The Twin"	(?) son of Alphaeus at Capernaum; a tax-collector
6. Certain religiously despised people - Lk 15.1	Mary Magdalene	Mk 15.40	Matthew		son of Alphaeus & Mary; (?) brother of Levi and Joses
	Mary, mother of James & Joseph	Mk 15.40	James	"The less"	

Table 6. Adherents of Jesus - Continued

Grouping or Types*	Named Individuals		"THE TWELVE"** Name	Other Name	Origin
7. Those saved by Jesus who followed him - Mk 10.52	Matthias	Acts 1.23	Thaddeus	Lebbaeus, (?) Judas	son of James
8. Those healed by Jesus who have "faith" - Lk 17.19	Salome	Mk 15.40	Simon	"The Zealot" or patriot;	
9. Relatives of the healed who also have "faith" - Mk 9.24	Simon of Bethany	Mk 14.3	Judas		Kerioth (Iscariot); "who betrayed Jesus"
	Simon the Pharisee	Lk 7.40			
10. John the Baptist's contingent - Lk 7.20,29	Susanna	Lk 8.3			
	Zacchaeus	Lk 19.8			
	Zebedee	Mk 3.17			

*Source: Baird, 1969, pp. 37-41, where all instances of each type are identified.

**Source: The listing is from Mk 3.16-19, Lk 6.14-16; Mt. 10-2-4; other information is from Barrett, 1970 & Goodspeed, 1957

observable physical circle of designated people around Jesus. They are the twelve disciples who came to be called "The Twelve" by some agency apart from Jesus' activity. Tradition has it that The Twelve are constant companions of Jesus, his closest circle and most intimate disciples, if not forming of themselves alone *the disciples* of Jesus. They were indeed disciples, and groups did indeed accompany Jesus. But they were not a group in Jesus' lifetime, at least; others too were disciples; and the membership of the groupings around Jesus varied as he went about. In the earliest material of the tradition, Jesus often appears alone; in the next he is stereotyped as surrounded by The Twelve (Conzelmann, 1973; also Bultmann, 1934).

Character of adherents

Although members of elite religious groups and other well-off, even plainly rich, people adhere to Jesus, his followers characteristically appear to be outcasts and others more lowly situated, especially the poor. Joachim Jeremias (1971, p. 112) summarizes his study of them as follows.

> Jesus' following consisted predominantly of the disreputable, the *amme ha-'ares* [Galileean people of the land], the uneducated, the ignorant, whose *religious* ignorance and *moral* behavior stood in the way of their access to salvation, according to the convictions of the time.

These are the people whom Jesus called *the poor*. They are, so he taught, invited by God to join in the festive meal of his Kingdom. "The Kingdom of God is yours!" he taught in actions (Mk 2.15) and words (Lk 6.20).

As was traditional, Jesus used the term poor in a comprehensive sense, as a rubric covering those in need generally, the variously oppressed, the hopeless, the desperate. He also added specifications (Jeremias, 1971). The poor as he sees them are the hungry and thirsty; the sick, the naked, and the stranger; those who weep, who labor, who bear heavy burdens; they are the last, the lost, the sinners, the simple, the least of all (e.g., Mt 11.28, 25.35-36). If the extent of this emphasis and aspiration in teaching were in empirical fact matched by a degree and quantity of response among people, then it was the poor who constituted the majority of his followers.

Like their number, the character of people *as disciples* is not to be specified. Disciples did nothing specific, and nothing specific marked them. Those physically about Jesus at any given time served as messengers, agents, servants, and helpers. Nothing otherwise distinguished them from other people. Disciples did not form a sect, follow a regulated lifestyle, teach a message or perform a specific activity. Disciples had no new or distinctive identity as a group, no name, no rite, sign, title or creed, no place to meet, no assembly before Jesus. Disciples were not a group that Jesus gathered about him, as the group of disciples, to receive special instruction--in "discipleship"--or to perform special activity as a disciple group (Conzelmann, 1973; Schweizer, 1971). No circle described the disciples as a group; and in any event, they would have nothing specific to do or be since Jesus did not teach specifics.

Discipleship in Jesus' lifetime seems to have been as unspecified in character as it was uncircumscribed in group and unrestricted in membership. The key to the *who* and the *what* of discipleship seems to be that which Jesus said as he gestured to those sitting around him: "Whoever does what God wants him to do" (Mk 3.35). The key to the *when* of discipleship is that which Jesus insistently taught of the arriving Kingdom and the departing world--it is here and now.

The eschatological character of Jesus' teaching finds complement in the eschatological character of discipleship. "The form of the present discipleship is the only one" (Conzelmann, 1973, p. 35). That makes understandable that Jesus did not instruct or train his disciples in any way of life or for any arena of later activity. For, there is no other stage to act upon than this present, last one. Teaching that the world was at an end and that God's ruling activity was breaking into the cosmos, Jesus could not also have taught a system of ethics (Bultmann, 1934), nor given instruction to his disciples (Guignebert, 1956), nor assign them to do anything specific, including imitating him (Schweizer, 1971), nor yet train them to live or to act something later (Conzelmann, 1973).

The same view appears when things are looked at from the other side. The very activity of the known disciples also shows them not to have formed a group receiving special instruction from Jesus in view of later life and activity. During Jesus' lifetime the disciples are not seen to form communities, to mirror Jesus' character, imitate his behavior, or memorize his sayings. After his death they are seen *not* to adopt his lifestyle, *not* to imitate him, and *not* to preserve and spread his teaching (Conzelmann, 1971). The disciples do not use his methods of teaching--parables, sayings, questions (Hinsdale, 1895). They do not teach only in Jewish milieux, as Jesus by conviction had. They do not teach or act as a group. The disciples use their own methods to teach their own subject matter with their own aim in various milieux: a teaching about Jesus, not the teaching of Jesus; and not about his life and character but about his death and transfiguration (e.g., Acts 3.13, 4.10, 5.30).

Along with The Twelve, Paul of Tarsus was one of the most prominent and successful apostles shortly after Jesus' death. Paul never made the slightest effort to expound Jesus' life or teachings. Indeed, he had never so much as met Jesus and he seems unaware of Jesus' words (Bornkamm, 1971, who notes that we know more about Jesus than Paul did). Paul taught the same formulas about Jesus as did Peter, one of the leaders of The Twelve (cf. I Cor 15.3-7 and Acts 2.32, 3.13-15).

Not of The Twelve, Paul regarded himself nonetheless as an apostle of Jesus (e.g., Gal 2.8). The apostles in the years just after Jesus' death were as uncircumscribed a group as they had been during his lifetime. The three fixed by tradition as Jesus' innermost circle of constant companions among the constant Twelve--Peter, James, John--are reflected in the three "Pillars" (Gal 2.9) among the apostles; these are Peter and John of The Twelve, together with a different James not of The Twelve; James was one of Jesus' brothers but not one of his disciples while Jesus lived. Along with Paul and the Pillars the apostles counted the original unspecified groups of Jesus' messengers and agents; the agents or apostles of the Jerusalem apostles and the apostles of Paul the apostle, together with the apostles of the various churches already formed around the eastern Mediterranean. This is the complication and confusion of apostolic affairs during the very first generation of "Christians" (Barrett, 1970)--as they only then came to be called (Acts 11.26). Something similarly kaleidoscopic appropriately describes the groupings of disciples scarcely twenty years earlier that had non-formed around Jesus as he went about teaching.

By the time that *Acts of the Apostles* was composed, some 60 years and more after Jesus' death, memory of early confusion and complication had faded or could no longer even be understood at such a remove (Bornkamm, 1971). In *Acts* Paul, once an apostle, is not an apostle, while The Twelve, once not apostles, are fixed as the apostles that Jesus had chosen and are depicted to assemble in Jerusalem to act days after his departing this life, along with Jesus' mother and brothers, who, not his disciples while he lived, now count in their company (Acts 1.12-14). Thereupon The Twelve disappear from view. Of Jesus' other disciples during his lifetime, there is little trace. In what therefore must discipleship have consisted during Jesus' lifetime?

Quite a different view of discipleship derives from the method of imagining the accomplishments of The Twelve long after Jesus' death, and then retroactively attributing to Jesus' teaching activity the aim that they should accomplish just that and the instruction and training to render them just so accomplished. On these grounds are based such classic and detailed works as *The Training of the Twelve* (Bruce, 1894), and others written from present evangelical or educational perspectives. *With Christ in the School of Disciple Building* (Wilson, 1976) exhibits Jesus' seven-step program of training the disciples to reproduce his ministry over the world. *The Master Plan of Evangelism* (Coleman, 1964) reproduces for today's training Jesus' detailed training of his disciples. Education writers identify as Jesus' objectives to prepare and train the disciples for service, imitation, and propagation throughout the world of Jesus' principles and way of life (Marquis, 1913; Piper, 1931; Tipsword, 1916). They identify the methods whereby he so trained them as the project method (Price, 1946; Roberts, 1955; Wilson, 1974), laboratory teaching (Marquis, 1913), and expression-work, "a whole series of carefully-graded exercises" (Shafto, 1923). Jesus is seen to have engaged the disciples as his teaching assistants, giving each one "a unique schedule of learning" so as to pass them from rustic Galileean to cosmopolitan leader (Richardson, 1931). He used them in team-teaching, the disciples handling the smaller seminars after his large lectures, undergoing "an extensive teacher-training course, including fieldwork, with the Master Teacher himself instructing them" (Wilson, 1974, p. 151). The Twelve were in Jesus' constant company as a traveling commune, learning by actively collaborating with him and by imitating his example and lifestyle (Grassi, 1978).

Yet on this present view The Twelve, far from being trained and accomplished performers, make but one appearance after Jesus' death and thereafter disappear in the main from the scene (save for Peter and John). "If the twelve had been the carefully chosen companions of Jesus on his journeys, they would not have been able so completely to disappear in the history of the young church, as in fact they did" (Schmithals, 1971, pp. 69-70). The performance of apostolic work was accomplished in the main by *other actors* who were not of The Twelve or any number of Jesus' disciples (e.g., Paul, James) and who had not been trained or even taught by Jesus in the flesh. The intimate circle of trained disciples is not seen to do the observed work; the work is seen to be done by a diffuse collection of untrained non-disciples.

The present view is grounded in the eschatological character of Jesus' teaching, in the history of the tradition's formation, and in the observation of apostolic activity. Knowledge and appreciation of some of these matters of text and evidence were not available to earlier modern writers, while alternative readings of text and evidence are always available. These account for some differences in understanding.

Other differences are accounted for by the aim and method of study. On the present view, Jesus as a teacher in his time cannot be understood by ascribing to him later or present-day aims and activities that are not to be found in his observed teaching activity or that are contravened by what is found in it. Nor can his learners at the time be understood by attributing to them a subsequent character and learning that can be seen to result from some agency other than Jesus' teaching activity and that cannot be seen during the time that he was teaching. These comments on method are made without prejudice to theological, religious, or devotional understandings of Jesus and present-day aspirations which may be served by some other view of things, but in favor of a pedagogical appreciation of Jesus as a teacher in his time, seen together with the learners of the time, the correspondents of his teaching.

The Question of Learning

The widest possible range of people in his milieu acted as correspondents to Jesus' teaching. By reason of their disposition, activity, and response, most people appear not to have learned what he taught. People of all kinds were opponents; people of all kinds were adherents. The question for adherents remains whether their--or whose among them--acceptance of the teaching was equivalent to *learning as taught*. A complementary question bears on what the opponents of Jesus, who learned neither what nor as he taught, did learn from the teaching-learning engagement. These questions point to a broader inquiry into *who learned what from the teaching*? That will lead to assessing the results in learning (see chapter 7) and thus the effectiveness or success of the teaching activity (chapter 8). But first: *how did Jesus teach?* (chapters 5 & 6)

Chapter 5

CONDUCT OF TEACHING

In actions and words Jesus taught this: The Kingdom of God is at hand. Repent! (Mk 1.15; Mt 4.17). How did his actions teach that?

No answer to this question will make any sense if it rests on familiar notions about teaching. What Jesus taught was not an informational subject-matter to be apprehended by intellectual processes; he did not teach at specialized times and places appointed for teaching to occur, nor to special people designated as recipients of teaching; and his performance of teaching was not comprised of a set of specialized behaviors reserved for the teaching act, time, place, and people. It is only barely possible to conceive of biology or 18th-century English literature being taught by the *actions* of the teacher--as Jesus taught "the Kingdom of God"; but it is easily conceivable that the Kingdom of God be taught in quite the same manner as biology and literature are taught. Jesus did not teach it that way. He taught it by actions. By which actions?

The answer, though comprehensible, is peculiar and alien to familiar ways of thinking about the world, for "the Kingdom of God" is a peculiar thing to teach and the actions by which Jesus taught it are familiar only to 1st century A.D. Palestinian Jewish ways of thinking and living. That the Kingdom of God was at hand betokened the dawning of God's ruling activity here and now, such that people had to do something about it here and now. Jesus taught this by his actions.

Teaching by Actions

Jesus taught the Kingdom of God by feasting in fellowship, by keeping bad company, by breaking the law, by healing the distressed, and by other *parabolic actions*. All of these are listed for convenient reference in Table 7.

These are actions that betokened or instantiated the Kingdom of God. Jesus also used words to betoken that, in parables. The parabolic actions may be followed by parabolic words, or not. The actions alone and of themselves did the teaching. To the actions may be accorded the pedagogical primacy, not only as they worked in Jesus' milieu but also as they hold with contemporary adage that actions speak louder than words. Hence, although Jesus surely taught by word and by deed, and although his word and deed surely accorded, he may be thought to have taught first by deed and then by word.

Only with furrowed brow do we and the people around us now come to see how Jesus' actions betokened the Kingdom of God. But it was as plain as day to the people around Jesus. They saw what he was teaching by feasting in fellowship; no one at the time could possibly mistake it. Most of them took immediate exception to the teaching.

Feasting in fellowship

Companionable eating and drinking at table was Jesus' habitual action. Feasting in hospitality with disreputable fellows, part of the habit, was his most significant parabolic action and the form of teaching the Kingdom of God that most impressed the people of his time (Jeremias, 1966, 1971). It was also the action that met with the sharpest of criticisms:

-- Look at this man! He is a glutton and a drinker, a friend of outcasts! (Mt 11.19)

-- This man welcomes outcasts and even eats with them! (L 15.2)

In complement to this parabolic action, Jesus might also tell a parable, more than likely at table. To justify his action before such criticism as giving

Table 7. Jesus' Teaching by Actions

FEASTING IN FELLOWSHIP	KEEPING BAD COMPANY	BREAKING THE LAW
1. giving hospitality - to outcasts: Mk 2.15-17; L 15.2 - to disciples: Mk 2.15-17, 14.22ff - generally Mk 6.41, 8.6-7	1. associating with outcasts a. feasting with them - as their guest: L 19.7 - as their host: Mk 2.15-17, L 15.2, Mt 11.19 b. receiving them as disciples - generally: L 15.1-2 - Levi: Mk 2.14 - Matthew: Mt 10.3 - Zacchaeus: L 19.8	1. feasting with outcasts Mk 2.15-17; L 15.2, 19.7; Mt 11.19 2. breaking the Sabbath Mk 2.23-28, 3.1-5; L 13.10-17. 14.1-6 3. blaspheming in claiming to forgive sins Mk 2.5-7; L 7.48
2. accepting hospitality - from outcasts: L 19.1-10 - from elites: L 7.36, 11.37, 14.1; Mk 14.3 3. using feasts in discourse - prayer: L 11.3-4 - parables L 14.7-11, 15-24 15.11-32, 16.19ff - sayings Mt 8.11; L 14.12-14, 16.22	2. associating with marginals a. women - receiving them as followers, disciples: Mk 15.40-41, 16.1, 9; L 8.2, 10.38-42 - showing them public compassion: Mk 7.25-30, 36-50, 12.41-44, 14.3-9; L 7.11-17 - touching & healing them: Mk 1.30-31, 5.25-35, 38-42, 16.9; L 13.10-13 b. children - welcoming, embracing, blessing, using them as example: Mk 9.36-37, 10.13-16 - healing them: Mk 5.38-42, 7.24-30, 9.17-27 c. unclean, lepers, possessed - welcoming, touching, healing (see list of healing, infra)	4. rejecting to fast Mk 2.18-22 5. rejecting to wash Mk 7.1-8

Table 7. Jesus' Teaching by Actions (continued)

HEALING THE DISTRESSED*		OTHER PARABOLIC ACTIONS**
1. curing the sick & disabled	1.	hospitality to outcasts: L 15.1f
- fever: Mk 1.29-31	2.	healings: (see list at left)
- leprosy: Mk 1.40-45; L 17.12-19	3.	rejection of fasting: Mk 2.19f
- lameness: Mk 2.1-12; Mt 8.5-13	4.	naming Simon "Peter": Mt 16.18
- consumption: Mk 3.1-6	5.	symbolic number (12) of disciples: Mk 3.14
- hemorrhage: Mk 5.25-34	6.	kingly entry into Jerusalem: Mk 11.1-10
- deafness & dumbness: Mt 9.32-34; L 11-14	7.	choice of ass to make entry: Mk 11.7
- blindness: Mk 8.22-36, 10.46-52; Mt 9.27-31; 12.22	8.	cleansing of the Temple: Mk 11.15-17
- epilepsy: Mk 9.14-29	9.	setting child in disciples' midst: Mk 9.36
- deformation: L 13.10-17	10.	washing disciples' feet: Jn 13.1ff
- dropsy: L 14.1-6	11.	writing in sand: Jn 8.6,8
2. exorcising the possessed & tormented	12.	weeping over Jerusalem: L 19.41-44
Mk 1.23-27, 32-34, 39, 3.11f, 14f., 22-27, 5.1-20, 6.7, 13, 7.24-30, 9.14-29, 38-40	13.	baptism by John: Mk 1.9
	14.	feeding crowds: Mk 6.32-44, 8.1-10
	15.	going to Jerusalem: Mk 10.33-34
	16.	cursing a fig tree: Mk 11.12-14
	17.	silence at trial: Mk 14.61, 15.5

* source: Jeremias, 1971, p. 86.
** source: 1-12 from Jeremias, 1966, p. 179;
13-17 from Stein, 1978, pp. 25-26.

hospitality to outcasts (L 15.2) he told a parable about going out to find the lost and then celebrating the find (vv. 4-6), and another (vv. 11-32) about the dead who are alive and the lost who are found--"Let us celebrate with a feast!" (v. 23). The Kingdom of God is a feast; everything usual is reversed; everyone is invited.

But what can any of that mean? In Jesus' milieu, it made all the difference who you ate with, for fellowship at table betokened fellowship before God and fellowship before God meant everything to decent, God-fearing people. Good people saw themselves fearfully obliged to avoid contact with bad people, above all not eating with them, and certainly not festively. Jesus ate with them, gladly. That meant the Kingdom of God.

> Jesus was having a meal in his house. A large number of tax collectors and other outcasts was following Jesus, and many of them joined him and his disciples at the table. (Mk 2.15)

Tax collectors and outcasts were by definition bad people, to the point of being denied civil rights--and quite rightly too, so convictions ran. Not only did Jesus not exclude these sorts of people but he actually gave them hospitality--at table, in his home, along with his other friends and followers. That action taught the Kingdom of God; it meant: "God invites you to his festive meal" (Jeremias, 1971).

Jesus hosted other sorts of people, too. He gave hospitality to his closer followers together with outcasts (Mk 2.15), and to a group of close followers at the Passover feast (Mk 14.22ff)--this was his supper. It was also his habit, so it seems, to give bread and fish to people generally who came to hear him (Mk 6.41, 8.6-7).

Jesus was guest as well as host. He honored disreputable people by accepting their hospitality, as with the tax-collector Zacchaeus. "This man has gone as a guest to the home of a sinner!" people said (L 19.7). What did that mean? The parabolic action finds complement in a parable (vv. 12-27), perhaps told at table, and a complementary saying about going to seek the lost (v.10).

Jesus feasted also with the elite. He accepted their hospitality, too. He ate Sabbath and other meals in the home of leading Pharisees and followers who were Pharisees (Mk 14.3; L 7.36, 11.37, 14.1). These above all other people made it a point to live rightly. One was Simon:

> A Pharisee invited Jesus to have dinner with him, and Jesus went to his house and sat down to eat. (L 7.36)

Somehow a woman known to be a sinner washed, dried, and perfumed Jesus' feet, occasioning Simon's criticism of Jesus. He thereupon told a parable about cancelling large debts and small (vv. 41-42), then told the woman: "Your sins are forgiven" (v. 48). This too occasioned criticism, far more severe. The actions are unmistakably plain. The festive meals in fellowship, with good and bad fellows, instantiate the Kingdom of God: they are forgiveness in action.

Feasting in fellowship as guest and host of friends and followers and onlookers, outcasts and elites, people good and bad, Jesus taught by action the Kingdom of God. It is a feast. Everyone is invited as fellows. Words could not make it clearer.

In complement to his parabolic action, Jesus used parabolic speech. His parables were told at the table (Trocme, 1973). He told of the Great Banquet and the Wedding Guest (L 14.7-11, 15-24), and other parables where, as was the case with feasting in fellowship, the lost are found, the dead are alive, big and small debts are cancelled, so feasts are celebrated. Who to invite? "When you give a feast, invite the poor, the crippled, the lame, and the blind" (L 14.13). The Kingdom of God is a feast (Mt 8.11, L 16.22). Jesus' feasting in fellowship taught the very same, by action.

The significance of this action can be appreciated by observing the fellowship meals of Jesus' followers and their converts after his death. There is first the fact that they observed the practice, sharing together in fellowship meals, eating with glad heart (Acts 2.42, 46, 20.7).

Next, trouble arose among them also over who was eating with whom in fellowship. Orthodox Jewish followers of Jesus severely criticized Peter for eating with non-Jewish followers of Jesus in Caesarea; the taunt recalls what had been thrown at Jesus: "You were a guest in the home of uncircumcised Gentiles, and you even ate with them!" (Acts 11.3). And in Antioch Paul publicly rebuked Peter for *ceasing* to eat with non-Jewish followers for fear of the Jewish ones; Peter and other Jewish followers who had been eating with non-Jewish ones were now acting like cowards and not true to the gospel (Galatians 2.11-14). This was one of the great crises that Jesus' followers struggled through early on, all but forgotten by the time of composing the gospel accounts (Bornkamm, 1971).

Lastly there is the fact, with a complex of meanings, that one kind of observance of the fellowship meal was literally called by Jesus' followers "the Lord's supper" (I Cor 11.33). Here too there is trouble about the fellowship: people who are better off are eating and drinking separately from others in the gathering; so "it is not the Lord's supper that you eat" (v. 20). There is recall to the last supper that Jesus had given, a Passover meal with his disciples before his death; and there is confession that when his followers feast in fellowship their action too, like his, betokens (v. 26)--though it betokens for them something else, Jesus' death. Finally, the relevant metaphor for Jesus' followers makes them as one body because they all share in the one loaf of bread (I Cor 10.17).

These practices and meanings--fraught otherwise with theological, evangelical, and liturgical significance--help to appreciate the historical facts that fellowship meals were an habitual action of Jesus; that a great deal depended on the fellows with whom he ate and drank; and that both the feasting and the fellowship betokened things of impressive significance to both friend and observer. From a pedagogical viewpoint, feasting in fellowship with all fellows was a teaching action of the very first order. And it was the central action of Jesus' teaching. It was an *acted parable* of the Kingdom of God (Perrin, 1967).

Keeping bad company

By the company he kept, Jesus taught both what the Kingdom of God is and who belongs in it. Status in the present scheme of things means nothing because the whole scene of activity is transforming. "The Kingdom of God is at hand." In this Kingdom are the good and right-living people and also the bad and wrongful ones, as well as the marginals in between.

In Jesus' milieu, beyond the circle of society lived the outcasts or pariahs. Among these were counted thieves, cheats, adulterers, prostitutes, the (religiously) ignorant and unclean, sinners and tax collectors (Mk 2.16; Mt 21.32; L 15.1, 18.11). Such people were well known not to keep the law, to engage in despicable occupations leading to immorality, and to be of such mind and behavior as to prevent their gaining salvation (Jeremias, 1971). These were the people to shun.

Jesus associated with these people. Not only did he not avoid them, he was notorious for welcoming their company and for accepting their friendship (Mt 11.19; L 15.2). As their honored guest and host, he feasted in fellowship with these disreputable and contemptible fellows, beyond even God's pale. He also taught them (L 15.1). And they counted among his followers and even his closest disciples. The names of three tax collectors are known as his disciples: Levi, Matthew, and Zacchaeus (Mk 2.14; Mt 10.3; L 19.8). Known not only to be morally foul, especially dishonest, and socio-politically repugnant, tax collectors or revenue contractors were literally outcast: they were outlawed, without civil rights, incompetent to give testimony in court. These were the kind of people whose company Jesus kept, to the point of making them his disciples.

Among the people within decent society but at its fringe were women and children. Jesus kept company with them also.

Women in Jesus' milieu were to be kept out of the heart of things public, if not in seclusion. They could not participate in the Temple cult, nor penetrate beyond its outer courts, and they could not give testimony at trials. Jesus associated with them by healing them and by otherwise publicly demonstrating sentiment towards them, and especially by receiving them as followers and disciples.

Jesus healed women with fever, deformity, hemorrhage, and possession (Table 7). As with his other healings, these acts incorporated the touching of the ritually unclean or otherwise shunned, if not dreaded, types.

In various ways, Jesus showed public compassion for women such as a widow at Nain, a Greek Syrophoenician woman, a prostitute, a poor widow, and a sinful woman (Table 7). These acts included public address and defense, and acceptance of touch--all surprising for being uncustomary and even abhorrent at the time, all the more so for a religious teacher.

Jesus counted women among his friends, his followers, and his disciples. A group of women accompanied him while he taught in Galilee and as he journeyed south to Jerusalem. Named among these are Mary Magdalene, Mary the mother of James and Joseph, Salome, Joanna, Susanna (Mk 15.40; L 8.2). He accepted their help, hospitality, and friendship; and he taught them, as he did Mary, Martha's sister (L 10.39). Notably not among them were Jesus' own mother and sisters, who were not his followers while he lived.

Children counted as little. The behavior of Jesus' disciples reveals the customary view:

> Some people brought children to Jesus for him to place
> his hands on them, but the disciples scolded the people.
> (Mk 10.13)

Jesus welcomed children. He healed boys and girls, he embraced them, and he blessed them (Table 7). In one particular parabolic action, he took a child and stood it in front of his disciples to rebuke their ambitioning (Mk 9.36). He also used children as an example of responding to the Kingdom of God (Mk 9.37, 10.15).

Breaking the law

Associating with outcasts, especially in festive meals, was one of Jesus' actions of breaking the law. He also broke laws concerning fasting, cleanliness, and the Sabbath, and he committed blasphemy in claiming to forgive sins (Table 7). Jesus even broke the Sabbath while teaching in synagogues and eating meals as guest in the home of leading Pharisees (Mk 3.1-5; L 13.10-17, 14.1-6). All of these actions merited in law death by stoning (Jeremias, 1971).

These actions gave great offense. Jesus was publicly challenged, criticized, and warned on their account. Each instance of these actions is presented as a "conflict story" or "controversy dialogue" (Hultgren, 1979; Bultmann, 1968), concluded by a saying of Jesus; the effect is to show Jesus' mastery at handling critical situations. He is known to have been executed for breaking some law (the official form of execution was as a criminal).

For uniting action and word, the act of forgiving sins (Mk 2.5; L 7.48) is unique among Jesus' parabolic actions. The words and the action are indistinguishable, forming a case that linguists call the use of a *performative* verb, as with "I promise" or "I'm warning you," where the action is accomplished by the utterance. That is not the case with other verbs such as "I am eating" or "I see you," which signal but do not at the same time accomplish the act they describe. The action of forgiving is accomplished by the uttering of "I forgive you." (For a specialized reason, this would customarily be cast in the Aramaic as the passive, "your sins are forgiven.") In Jesus' case this action, far from being regarded as benign, was observed with perplexity and indignation (Mk 2.6, 12; L 7.49). It was blasphemy, not kindliness, and it was indictable.

What was Jesus teaching by his parabolic actions of breaking the law? Each instance may have had its own lesson, as in the doing of good even on the Sabbath (Mk 3.4; L 13.15-16). But the instances and the specifics are never at issue in Jesus' teaching. Common to all cases is the teaching, not to break the law--itself only a thematic instance--but to act decisively in face of the dawning reign of God. The things that matter don't matter, all is reversed.

The parables that Jesus spoke are pictures of action in the face of critical situations; like the situations, they demand immediate, decisive behavior in response. The Kingdom of God means: "God is near. It is the critical hour. Everything is at stake. Act now!" (paraphrase of Jeremias, 1966, 1971). That is what Jesus' parabolic actions teach, rather than teaching the specificity of that behavior which is involved, as an accident, in this and that circumstance of his action.

Thus, Jesus' action of feasting with outcasts does not teach the specific behavior of inviting outcasts to your table, and his feasting with elites does not teach catering to elites; nor does it teach to give banquets and live it up. The parabolic form runs: *It is the case with the Kingdom of God as it is the case with feasting in fellowship* (paraphrase of Jeremias, 1966). His parabolic actions taught the Kingdom of God; they did not teach to include or to exclude outcasts or elites while feasting--the whole distinction, so essential at the time, no longer mattered. The world as known is ending; what matters is radical decision, decisive action, in face of an upending world.

This is the sort of action depicted in Jesus' spoken parables, too, just as it was betokened in his parabolic actions. The words complement the actions. In the series of parables that Jesus told about servants, all of them show servants taking action; in half of them the good servants are rewarded, while in the other half the bad servants are rewarded (Crossan, 1973). An estate manager about to be dismissed rigs the accounts to make friends of debtors, and the owner whom he cheats praises him (L 16.1-7). He is a criminal, but he is a model of decisive action in a critical hour. Other well-known story parables of Jesus all depict similar reversals, polar reversals where the good are bad and the bad good (Crossan, 1973): the Good Samaritan--the title itself a contradiction in terms--the Rich Man and Lazarus, the Pharisee and the Publican, the Wedding Guest, the Great Supper, and the Prodigal Son (L 10.30-36, 16.19-26, 18.10-14, 14.7-11, 16-24, 15.11-32). As with the first who become last and the last who become first, the good are bad and the bad are good. Such antithetical parallelisms are of the very essence of Jesus' parabolic words and actions, and of the Kingdom of God that his actions and words taught.

Healing the distressed

By his healing actions, Jesus taught that the Kingdom of God was coming in. It is a simple lesson and the teaching of it is stunning. The actions taught that Satan's rule is over and God's rule is beginning. Here is a perfection of message in action, and perfect complement of parabolic actions and words.

In Jesus' milieu, it was well known that dark personal forces of evil lay behind the awful suffering of dreaded disease and torments. And it was on that precise account of evil that the possessed and leprous, for example, were if at all possible to be avoided. Jesus did not shy from them. He touched them. By curing the sick and by exorcising the possessed, he taught that the ruling of evil forces was over and done with.

These healing actions brought criticism from sophisticates as well as astonishment from other observers. Jesus was criticized not for healing, but for healing on the Sabbath (Mk 3.2; L 13.14, 14.1). He was criticized not for the fact of exorcising, nor for its success, but for its source: he did it by the power of the devil, some people said, an evil spirit within him (Mk 3.22, 30). To his friends it was "doing good," healing those under the devil's power because God was with him (Acts 10.38). The action was plain enough; its source was in dispute. Jesus himself appeared to take it as the beginning of God's ruling activity. Beyond that he made nothing of it.

Nor did anyone else make much of it at the time. In Jesus' milieu it was well known that "miracles could happen," and people enough were known to effect them. What may have struck the eye was not the event in itself but its character, and the characteristic way in which Jesus conducted himself. For, this aspect of Jesus' conduct as a teacher exhibited systematic differences from the miracle workers and miracle stories circulating in the Judaic, Hellenistic, and Roman milieux (Leaney, 1966; Sabourin, 1972; Trocme, 1973; Voegtle, 1971).

No doubt Jesus' contemporaries could have noted in the first place that he demanded no payment or return for the healing, appeared to derive no "personal" profit or benefit from the act, and based no status claims on it, whether for himself or his teaching.

It was also notable that the people who benefitted from these acts were ordinary, sick, and otherwise not well-off individuals--not the rich and privileged, not the masses, and not Jesus himself.

People may also have wondered over the fact that the acts were beneficial to begin with--never punitive, destructive, or malevolent; no spectacular or stupefying demonstrations of effect, exhibitions of prowess, or transmogrifications of a mild-mannered but put-upon personage with secret devastating powers.

Everything about the event is *realistic*--the setting, the occasion, the people, the conduct. There are no bizarre or grotesque features, no curiosities, burlesque, fantasy, portents; not even trances, visions, states or dreams. The depiction does not strike as inventive but descriptive of a precise historical context. Where is the P.R. man? we may wonder today. Where is Cecil B. De Mille to render the proper theatrical effect?

Above all, the act is realistic in execution. Jesus never heals or exorcizes by *iatromantic* or magical means (Sabourin, 1972) but by simple gesture and word. He engages in no complicated practices, operations, or treatments. There are no accoutrements, no paraphernalia, accessories, props or charms. There is nothing at all occult, no incantation or ritual; and no magical intervention is produced in result.

Like other actions and words of Jesus, these healing acts are direct assertions, self-authoritative.

With respect to their place in his teaching, the curative actions of Jesus were perceived by contemporaries as a noteworthy but not exceptional component. Exorcisms and healings were a culturally accepted part of the activity of religious teaching and of the identity of a religious teacher (Robbins, 1984). To today's eyes these events are extra-ordinary, particularly so in the activity of teaching; and what is most striking is that these so-perceived extraordinary events play *no more* than an ordinary role. Nothing much is made of them--not by Jesus, not by the gospel texts. No teaching of Jesus and no status for Jesus is made to depend on the miracles--not by Jesus himself, not by the texts. The healings and exorcisms take their place among other events. They seem ordinarily situated and occasioned, relatively few and unsalient. Indeed, they are trifling in number and effect when compared to the misery all around (Schweizer, 1971).

Why?--some may ask--did Jesus not wipe out the mass misery instead of alleviating only an individual here and there? The question is a carping one. Others might ask: why did Jesus not throw the Romans into the sea? Indeed, why did he not free the slaves?--clean up corruption, codify law, endow universities, electrify the countryside, equalize income, provide affordable housing, get criminals off the streets? The question is also a misconceived one, misconceiving Jesus and his teaching. The answer serves to recall what Jesus' teaching was.

Jesus had, it seems, no interest in making the world a better place in which to live. For one thing, he was convinced that it was at an end. But above all he was interested in the will of God. He had no concern to relieve mass misery but to teach the coming Kingdom of God. It did not matter whether misery or delight surrounded. It made no difference whether an individual lay in suffering or reclined in opulence, just as it did not matter whether the individual were he or she, outcast or elite, first or last, and the rest. Jesus may have shown compassion here and there, but everywhere he showed a consuming passion for God's Kingdom and a single-minded pursuit of teaching people *that.*

It is rather the people who did not share such passion and pursuit who worried themselves over the morrow. And it is people like us, living in the morrow, who come to wonder why it is that Jesus did not concern himself with being, doing, and teaching something other than he was, did, and taught.

For instance, it is perplexing to see Jesus not devote himself to relieving people's sufferings, just because he was whole-heartedly devoted to teaching the Kingdom of God. Why couldn't he take some time out to heal some of the other sick people too?--they have just as much right to a better life. Just because he thought the world was coming to an end doesn't mean he couldn't have used his powers to help make this world a better place to live. Also, maybe if people could have had their basic needs taken care of, then they might have paid more attention to what Jesus was saying about God. Just because he put God first doesn't mean that he couldn't have tried to put other people first--especially the people who really needed him, like the poor and the hungry and the political prisoners. And what about abortion?

Why indeed did Jesus not think ahead and work towards the betterment of this world with all of its problems, instead of thinking it was at an end and working all the time for the Kingdom of God? This contemporary perplexity shows itself nowhere more acute than on the question of Jesus' miracles. All that power! What a waste.

The answer is that Jesus did not have all that power, nor did he waste it. The powers that he did have were exhausted in teaching the Kingdom of God. All of the healings that Jesus performed, few as they were and restricted in kind, befitted his teaching. They are *eschatological* in character. He does no other kind, and few enough of these.

Healings and exorcism are one of the actions by which Jesus taught people the Kingdom of God. That is what--and it is exhaustively what--he set out to teach. Both the action itself and Jesus' conduct of it served to condign purpose--teaching the Kingdom of God. Satan's ruling is over! God's ruling activity is beginning! Repent now!

People in Jesus' time but not in ours could see these actions teaching that plainly enough, and they could appreciate why the teacher did just that and not something else. Naturally, they needn't have agreed with the teaching but they had no trouble getting the point of what was being enacted before their eyes. Today it is easy to miss the point as well as to disagree with the teacher, with the way he chose to make his point, and with the point that he chose to make.

Other parabolic actions

Numerous individual actions of Jesus that do not figure in the thematic actions reviewed here have been identified as parabolic by Jeremias (1966) and Stein (1978)--see Table 7. As with all such actions, "the teaching was nonverbal and contained in the action itself" (Stein, p.25).

Other scholars also treat of Jesus' parabolic actions.

> The conduct of Jesus is 'message,' as much as his words; they are inseparable and consistent. ... Jesus' actions are not just illustrations of his message, they *are* his message. (Stanton, 1974, pp. 152, 166)

The Kingdom of God, says Schillebeeckx (1979), was given substantive content by Jesus' actions: miracles; dealings with tax collectors and sinners; fellowship at table with friends; attitude towards the Law, Sabbath, and Temple; and consorting in fellowship with disciples. Jesus talks about the coming rule of God, "while at the same time his life is a striking parable of it" (p. 170). The teacher as doer is noted by Grassi (1978), with Jesus acting first and expressing it in proverbs and parables (pp. 64, 67). Stevens (1901) directly identified "actions" as one of Jesus' methods of teaching, along with parables and sayings.

* * *

The question arises whether this is a case of teaching by example. Biblical scholars (Stein, 1978) and educational writers are unanimous in according the highest praise to Jesus as a teacher for embodying what he taught. His teaching method included giving a living demonstration and serving as exemplar--"He lived what he taught" (Bennion, 1981; Horne, 1920; Kealy, 1978; McKoy, 1930; Richardson, 1931; Russell, 1944) and teaching by example--"Jesus himself practiced what he preached" (Hubery, 1970; Jones, 1957). On that view, Jesus proposed things for people to do and then showed them how to do it, demonstrating it before them or providing an edifying example in his own life. On the one side is his teaching; on the other, his conduct--his merit is to have conducted himself according to his own teaching.

To the contrary, Jesus was not a teacher who teaches by example. He does not practice what he preaches, he does not live what he teaches; more accurate to say that Jesus *preached what he practiced* and *taught what he lived*. Jesus taught by actions. His actions are what he teaches, not an example of something that he teaches.

From a pedagogical viewpoint, the thing that Jesus teaches is taught by actions *and* it is taught by words; actions and words find complement in one another; both of them teach the same "message," the Kingdom of God, through different modalities. The actions do not stand apart from the message, and they do not operate differently from the words; the actions betoken the Kingdom of God, and the words betoken the Kingdom of God.

The view proposed here rearranges familiar emphases on word and deed, teaching and example, in favor of a more powerful conception of a teacher who was a man of original, self-authoritative, and urgent action and speech. Jesus taught in deed, then word; what he did was what he taught. His words taught that, too. The actions are not examples of the words, and the words are not illustrations of the actions. His two ways of teaching one and the same thing, the Kingdom of God, are each of them condign with what was being taught, and complementary one with another: actions and words, both are parables of the Kingdom of God.

Conduct as a Teacher

How did Jesus conduct himself as a teacher? In what manner did he perform the actions of teaching?

From a pedagogical viewpoint, Jesus' conduct can be seen as unregulated by constraints of place, time, people, system, and other commonplace curricular considerations. On these accounts his teaching conduct is characterized by non-formality, variety, and originality. It can otherwise be seen as governed by constraints of the subject-matter and the aim or purpose of teaching it. On these accounts Jesus' teaching conduct is characterized by authority, immediacy, and above all, by urgency.

Jesus conducted the activity of teaching without regard to time, place, and people in their character as designates of teaching activity. It didn't matter whether they were so designated or not; he taught as designated and as undesignated.

Places designated for teaching activity included the synagogue, the Temple, and the room or locale most readily understood as classroom. Jesus taught in these places. He also taught in other places--in the open, along the way, in houses, at table. The time of his teaching activity included the times appointed for it in places designated for it (as in the synagogue), and also unappointed times, elsewhere as so happened; and its durations exceeded the designated teaching period by being a constant or chronic activity rather than an intermittent or chronological one--the hour of teaching was all the time, moreso than for a time.

Place and time show Jesus not to sit and wait but to go out and about as he engaged in teaching. Teaching happened as occasion presented itself and as circumstance could be turned to occasion. Occasion included people to teach. People presented themselves for the occasion and Jesus presented himself to them for an occasion. Going as he did out and about, Jesus taught people as they were found; and quite distinctively, it was he who called them to associate in the teaching activity: "Come, learn this from me," as it were.

As distinctively, the people called or welcomed to the teaching activity included all types, not solely that type commonly designated as student. In Jesus' conduct of teaching, people acted in complement to his teaching activity, in the occasion of time, place, and activation of the teaching; the character of learner or student accrued to them in the occasion rather than by prior designation. Thus Jesus particularly did not teach only those characterized as disciples; he is seen to teach onlookers and opponents as well. He teaches women as well as men; outcasts as well as elites and marginals; the casual and the close; crowds, groups, and individuals. All of these are participants in his teaching activity as he conducted it, playing the role of learners to his teacher. Most of them did not learn what he taught.

Unregulated by constraints of time, place, and people, Jesus' conduct as teacher was disciplined by the subject matter that he taught and the reason for teaching and learning it. "The Kingdom of God is near. Repent!" In that relation, his teaching activity takes its distinctive character of sure, immediate, and urgent conduct.

Jesus' conduct as a teacher was self-authoritative. He does not act as directed. He does not deliver or interpret established texts, laws, doctrines, opinions or positions from anyone else, nor as authorized by anyone else. He acts of his own, with no reference to any source of his teaching conduct.

The conduct of teaching is immediate. It is not aloof or removed from the people before him, the time and place they occupy, nor the matter at hand there and then. His conduct is here and now, in direct address. He does not say, "Thus it is written" or "Thus saith the Lord" but "I say" and "I say to you." He does not heal by incantation and ritual but by direct touch and simple directive. His teaching is an act of assertion in deed and in word.

This asserting is vehement. Jesus' conduct is above all insistent and pressing. He acts as though the people before him stood with their backs at the brink of the world. It is the end; what is coming now is the reigning of God. In face of the end and in face of God, act. The learning of this is urgent, and the teaching of it is urgent. Who learned it?

Chapter 6

LANGUAGE OF TEACHING

Jesus taught in words as well as deeds. How did he use language to teach? Considered as pedagogical activity, Jesus' language is seen to complement the actions by which he taught the Kingdom of God. But although he taught primarily by deeds, then by words, later generations have always paid more attention to his words -- e.g., his story parables more so than his parabolic actions. Words have become the primary medium for representing thought or content; the form in which we have Jesus' teachings is verbal, moreover not oral but written; and scholars have devised sophisticated ways of studying words and texts.

For these commonplace reasons we know far more about Jesus' language than his actions of teaching. We no longer see him teach, nor even hear him; we read his teachings. His language has been studied vastly more extensively, and examined more minutely, than his actions of teaching; and it has been studied primarily for theological or devotional rather than pedagogical aspects. Our interest here is in the pedagogical function of Jesus' language. How did Jesus make use of language while teaching? In what respects did his language serve to teach?

The first half of the chapter describes his language, the second half evaluates it as a medium of teaching. Our first effort will be to hear him teach, by describing the *tongue* which he spoke and the *sound* of his teaching. Next we describe the *structure* and *forms* of his language. Then we evaluate its *rhetorical qualities* and lastly identify some *issues* that remain in question about his language as a teaching device.

On the whole, the way in which Jesus used language to teach shows impressive congruence among its sound, structure, form, and content. That shows mastery of language, but more pointedly it shows masterly use of language to teach. As with the actions by which Jesus taught, the language too befits the subject being taught through it, while actions and words also befit one another.

The Tongue

Of the four major languages used in the Palestine of his day, Jesus was familiar with three. These three are not the Hebrew-Latin-Greek of the notice posted at his execution (Jn. 19.20), for Jesus knew nothing of Latin, whereas his native language did not figure in the notice. Jesus' mother tongue was Aramaic, and it was in Aramaic that he spoke and taught (as demonstrated by Dalman, 1902). He could read and probably speak Hebrew, and he could probably understand and speak some Greek. But although aware of Latin, Jesus could not have known it, as Latin was almost exclusively restricted to the Roman army; even among themselves the auxiliaries of the region would use a familiar language such as Greek or Syriac--a branch of Aramaic--and it was likely in one of these languages that the Herodian/Roman officer conversed with Jesus about his sick servant (Mt. 8. 5-13).

Greek & Hebrew

Greek and Hebrew were, at most, Jesus' second languages (cf. Dalman, 1929; Fitzmyer, 1979). For a number of reasons Greek had come to be widespread in the general area of Palestine, and particularly in Galilee (e.g., due to Herod's Hellenizing projects). Galilee was the province of Jesus' origin and major teaching activity. His home village, Nazareth, was situated near Hellenistic towns and at their crossroads; Jesus passed through Greek-speaking districts (e.g., Hippos); and some of his closest associates, also Galileans, bore Greek names (e.g., Philip and Andrew). [Of course, multiple names were common enough, as with the one disciple known by Hebrew, Aramaic, and Greek names of Simon, Cephas, and Peter.] Thus Jesus lived and moved in an area of Hellenic influence and he, like many others, certainly heard Greek spoken. Gustaf Dalman concluded that it is not credible, and it is even impossible, that Jesus should not have understood

Greek (1929, p. 6). Joseph Fitzmyer concludes that the evidence for Jesus' use of Greek "yields at most a probability" (1979, p. 37).

To be sure, Aramaic rather than Greek remained the most commonly used language of the people and the land, but by no means was Greek used only by non-Jews. "Many Palestinian Jews, not only those in Hellenistic towns, but farmers and craftsmen of less obviously Hellenized areas used Greek, at least as a second language" (Fitzmyer, 1979, p. 46). Immigrant Greek-speaking Jews had their own synagogues in Palestine, even in Jerusalem; Greek was the language of cultural and commercial exchanges with foreigners; and the Roman officials in Palestine, as elsewhere, carried on their affairs in Greek (Dalman, 1929). Thus Pilate may well have spoken to Jesus in Greek (Mk. 15.2), as also the Canaanite woman (Mk. 7. 26) who in language was Greek. We can therefore think that Jesus knew at least enough Greek to get by.

As for Hebrew, it had long before the time of Jesus become a literary and liturgical language, no longer a popular tongue. Yet it was cultivated in learned circles (Black, 1967, p. 15), and it was still being spoken in various geographical pockets or social strata (Fitzmyer, 1979, p. 45). Although Jesus himself was known to be uneducated and ignorant--i.e., not learned--he had surely learned to read Hebrew, probably as part of his religious training when a youth. He could read the Hebrew scriptures, and read them aloud, as when he stood to read from them in the synagogue services prior to delivering his discourse (Lk. 4. 16-21). On that point, Dalman (1929, pp. 9-10) stresses that it had become necessary to follow the Hebrew reading with an oral translation in the vernacular Aramaic or Greek, so that worshippers could understand it.

In addition to his reading knowledge, Jesus appears to have been able to speak Hebrew, that is, the learned language. He certainly engaged in many public disputations and dialogues in the rabbinical style, when his knowledge would be tested, his teaching contested, and his opinion sought (see Dillon, 1981b). As depicted in the gospels, these exchanges exhibit the technical methods and terms of the rabbinical schools and they perhaps as well transpired in rabbinical Hebrew (Manson, 1935, p. 50; Black, 1967, p. 49). If these exchanges did in fact take place in Hebrew, we have yet to account for their verbal translation into the gospel traditions. For example, who among

Jesus' associates were present who could have understood and recounted the exchanges as we know them? Perhaps interested parties (people like today's court-watchers) habitually gave bystanders a running translation or a summary after the fact. In any event, it is clear that Jesus was familiar with Hebrew.

Aramaic

It was in Aramaic, his native language and the popular tongue, that Jesus conversed and taught (Dalman, 1902, 1929; Black, 1967; Jeremias, 1971). The language which Jesus spoke belonged to the Western branch of the Aramaic family of languages. His own tongue was a Galilean version of Western Aramaic, a dialect sufficiently different in certain aspects of pronunciation, vocabulary, and grammar from the Aramaic in Judea to the south (Dalman, 1902, pp. 79-82; Jeremias, 1971, p. 4) as to distinguish a Galilean in Jerusalem. The Galilean way of speaking Aramaic was just the sign by which Jesus' associates are depicted to have been recognized at the time of his arrest (Mt. 26.73). Presumably, Jesus himself could be recognized to speak Galilean Aramaic.

As part of his conclusive demonstration that Aramaic was Jesus' mother tongue, Gustaf Dalman (1902, *passim*, 1929, pp. 11-14) cited the words of Jesus left in Aramaic (with translation added) by the gospel tradition. For example, Jesus is depicted to say *itpattah*, open up, when healing a deaf-mute (Mk. 7.34), and when healing a girl, *talyeta kumi*, little girl get up (Mk. 5.41). There are the Aramaic names or nicknames of Jesus' associates, such as *kepha* for Peter the rock, *toma* for Thomas the twin, *bene regesh* for the sons of rage James and John. And Jesus is addressed in Aramaic by a blind man and by Mary Magdalen who called him *rabbuni*, rabbi, sir (Mk. 10.51; Jn. 20.16). A more expansive list of two dozen and more Aramaic words on Jesus' lips--omitting all personal and place names--has been devised by Joachim Jeremias (1971, pp. 4-7). Some familiar words which Jesus says are *reqa*, *mamona*, and *'abba*--fool, money, father (Mt. 5.22, 6.24; Mk. 14.36). His dying words are given in Aramaic (Mt. 27.46). Jeremias further points to Aramaic idioms alien to Hebrew and Greek, as in the Lord's Prayer (Mt. 6.12); and he uncovers variants and mistranslations of Aramaic into the Greek of the gospels, as in the story of the repentant woman where Jesus is translated to say "since I came into the house," instead of "since *she* came in" (Lk. 7.45).

Knowledge of the fact that Jesus spoke Aramaic is of importance from several points of view. Significant historical as well as theological interest attaches to the tongue which Jesus spoke, and not only to what it was that he said but also to the way in which, and to the linguistic setting in which, he said (and thus meant?) it. For our purposes here we will emphasize--to the extent that the distinction is possible--the rhetorical aspects of Jesus' Aramaic speech, with a view to its pedagogical function, not its theological implications in themselves.

Our interest is to understand Jesus' language as part of his pedagogy. We therefore examine the forms of his speech in relation to the content of his teaching. Examined in this light, Jesus' way of speaking *in Aramaic* reveals a fruitful perspective on Jesus as a teacher--a perspective which remains altogether hidden from view when his language is read in Greek, still more when it is read in English, and all the more when it is read rather than heard. We will therefore try first to hear him teach.

The Sound

We are not Aramaic-speaking Jews, we do not live in early 1st-century Palestine, and we do not stand in face of the urgently speaking Jesus. But we can come to appreciate something of the sound of his teaching thanks to the scholarship of Gustaf Dalman, Matthew Black, and Joachim Jeremias (among others).

Jesus' distinctive way of speaking can be seen in his prayer. "Father," he begins--in an unusual usage of *'abba*--and now Dalman (1929, p. 20) gives us the Aramaic:

> *'abba,*
> *kulla yakhel lak,*
> *a'bar minni hada kasa,*
> *beram la ma desabena*
> *ana ella ma deatt sabe.* (Mk. 14.36)

(Throughout we give the transliterated version and omit diacritical markings.) Even through our ignorance and remoteness we can perceive in these words a kind of repetition, rhythm, and structure. These aspects characterize Jesus' way of speaking.

Repetition of Sounds & Words

Repetition of sounds and word-play in particular were discovered by Matthew Black to be a regular feature of Jesus' teaching in his native Aramaic (1967, pp. 276-277). These features disappeared in Greek translation--not to mention the English version of the Greek. When the Greek is translated back into Aramaic, there reappear the alliteration, assonance, and paronomasia characterizing Jesus' sayings.

Let us start with some examples of Jesus' puns, a form of paronomasia, for these will be easy enough for us to appreciate. At one point Jesus criticized religious purists for straining a gnat out of their drink yet swallowing a camel (Mt. 23.24). The pun appears when we substitute the Aramaic words in play:

You strain a *galma*, but swallow a *gamla*!

The example permits us to notice a fascinating aspect of Jesus' language. We already know that this sentence--even in English--delivers a striking image by juxtaposing the two terms of straining a gnat and swallowing a camel. Now we learn from the Aramaic that the juxtaposition is doubly striking, for both images and sounds are juxtaposed. In another instance Jesus retorts to critics by saying (Lk. 14.5):

If any of you had
a *bera* or a *be'ira* (son, ox)
fall into a *bera*, (pit)
would you not pull him out on the sabbath?

One of the sayings about treasures (Lk. 12.33) is another example of paronomasia:

Lay up treasures in heaven,
where no thief can *qarebh* (get near)
and no *ruqba* can *marqebh.* (moth, corrupt)

(We insert the Aramaic words into English syntax only as a presentational device, to aid us in appreciating the word-play.)

In all, Black cites some three dozen instances of alliteration, assonance, and paronomasia (1967, pp. 160-185), grouping them by predominance of laryngals and palatals, sibilants and palatals, and dentals and labials. The parable of the mustard seed is a good example (Mk. 4.31-32):

The Kingdom of God is like this.	
A man *zera'* a mustard seed,	sows
which is *ze'er*	less
than all *zar'in.*	seeds
But when it *rebhi,*	grows
it is *rabba*	greater
than all *zero'in.*	herbs

A particularly impressive instance of congruence of sound and image is Jesus' saying about the lilies of the field (Mt. 6.28-29):

Consider the *shushanin,*	lilies
how they *shabhehin.*	grow
Not even *Shelomoh*	Solomon
in his *teshbohteh*	glory
was arrayed like these.	

Here we have an utterance of surpassing fittingness, where softness and grace of sound give image to flowery and kingly finery. Another instance is Jesus' evocative call, "Come to me, all you who labor, and I will give you rest" (Mt. 11.28-30), where in Aramaic "the prevailing sounds are all soft, smooth, and pleasant" (Black, 1967, p. 183).

These few examples may be enough for us to appreciate a striking feature of Jesus' language. In the Aramaic, Jesus' utterances are

> cast in a medium which can express in appropriate and modulated sound the underlying beauty of the sentiment or the passion out of which the thought arose--soft and gentle in the kindly sayings, as in the promise to the heavy-laden, inexorable and hard in the sayings about Offences, strongly guttural and mockingly sibilant where hypocrites and 'the rest of men' are contrasted with the Christian disciples. (Black, 1967, p. 185)

This powerful and suggestive finding leads us to conclude that not only is the image or content of Jesus' saying appropriate to the audience or purpose, but also the *sound* is appropriate to both image and purpose.

Rhythm & rhyme

A similar conclusion holds for the rhythm and rhyme of Jesus' sayings. These aspects of sound too are lost in the Greek translation. (Although the Greek itself may exhibit a certain rhythm and rhyme.) They are recovered for us by Joachim Jeremias (and C. F. Burney, 1925) who cites four dozen and more instances grouped in four different rhythmic patterns (1971, pp. 20-27). Just as Black's groupings had revealed that Jesus' repetition of particular sounds accorded with the particular image and purpose of the saying, so Jeremias finds that sayings with different contents and purposes are cast in different rhythms.

The 2-beat rhythm requires terse and abrupt formulations, thus lending them an urgency which well befits their use for Jesus' central ideas. Examples include these instructions to messengers (Mt. 10.8):

'al mag*gan* qabbel*tun*
'al mag*gan* ha*bun*

and the command to love one's enemies (Lk. 6.27):

raha*mun* leba'ale debabe*kon*
tayye*bun* lesane'e*kon*.

The 4-beat rhythm (and 4+4+2) is found in sayings addressed to disciples, as for example the "salt of the earth" saying (Mk. 9.50):

'in milh*a* tap*el*
bem*a* tetabbe*lun*.

That saying is also a play on words--*tapel/tabbel*, salt/season. Jesus' famous prayer, the Lord's Prayer (Mt. 6.9-13), is in 4-beat rhythm. C. F. Burney (1925) renders it as a little poem or hymn in two stanzas of 4-beat tristichs (pp. 113, 161), with "a remarkably elaborate system of rhyme" (p. 162):

'abunan debismayya	--	yitkaddas semak
tete malkutak		tehe sibyonak
hekma debismayya		hekden be'ar'a
lahman deyoma	--	hab lan yoma den
usebok lan hoben		hek disbaknan lehayyaben
wela ta'linan lenisyona		'ella passinan min bisa.

The most frequently found rhythm is the 3-beat, serving to express important sayings (e.g., Mt. 8.20). The Beatitudes (Mt. 5.3-11) are, in the main, in 3-beat rhythm with rhyme. For example, here are the first two Beatitudes (as rendered by Burney, 1925, p. 166):

1. tubehon miskenayya [beruha]
   dedilehon malkuta dismayya.

2. tubehon demit'abbelin
   dehinnun mitnahhamin.

The joining of 3-beat and 2-beat rhythms into the *kina* (dirge) meter serves to express strong inner emotion, as in the saying about the bad servant (Mt. 24.48):

han dihwe pu*g*ra
mitkanne*s*in nisra*y*ya

and the saying about the last shall be first (Mt. 20.16):

ye*hon* 'ahra*ye* qadma*in*
weqadma*ye* 'ahra*in*.

All of these selected examples show rhyme as well as rhythm.

What may we conclude about the sound of Jesus' teaching? A generalization from these examples to the whole of Jesus' speech is impermissible. But we can say that to a significant extent the sound of his sayings--their rhythm and rhyme, their alliteration, assonance, and word-play--is suited in an impressively fine way to both the image and the purpose of expression, at very least in the some 100 instances revealed by Black, Burney, Dalman, and Jeremias.

The Structure

The most characteristic structure of Jesus' sayings is parallelism of members. That is, part B of a saying parallels part A, as in:

A. The first will be last, and
B. the last will be first. (Mt. 20.16)

It is this feature, together with his imagery, which leads most authors to speak of the "poetry" of Jesus' sayings; indeed, C. F. Burney first described the parallelism in *The Poetry of Our Lord* (1925). The parallel structure is not unique to Jesus, for it is found in the Jewish tradition. But parallelism unmistakably characterizes Jesus' sayings and it is evident even in their English version.

The parts of a saying can parallel one another in various ways, such as when part B is opposite to A, or synonymous with A. *Antithetical* parallelism is the type most frequently found in Jesus' sayings. No fewer than 138 instances from the synoptic gospels are listed by Jeremias (1971, pp. 15-16), along with numerous instances of seven different ways in which the A vs. B antithesis is achieved: by word-opposition, by negation, by question-statement contrast, by polarization, complementarity, inversion, and by combination of opposition and negation. "We may speak of a preference for antithetical parallelism on the part of Jesus" (p. 20). Jeremias has also pointed out (pp. 18-19) that one of the distinctive features of Jesus' own usage of parallel structure is that the second member bears the stress, whereas in Old Testament parallelisms the stress is on the first member. The following saying, for example (Mt. 23.12), becomes a word of encouragement by reason of stress on the second member, rather than the threat it would be if the first were stressed:

A. Whoever exalts himself will be humbled, and
B. whoever humbles himself will be exalted.

This saying represents as well an example of antithetical parallelism achieved by the device of inversion.

Instances of other types of parallelism in Jesus' sayings have been cited by many authors, although some of the instances could as well be classified as antithetical. Table 8 lists five types together with one example for each.

The examples in Table 8 can be manipulated a bit further to illustrate some of the workings of parallel structure. The climactic example (Mk. 9.37) can be diagrammed as:

B. welcomes the one
who sent me.
↑
B. welcomes me; and —— a. whoever welcomes me

a. Whoever welcomes ↑
one of these children,

Table 8. Parallel Structure of Jesus' Sayings*

PARALLELISM	EXAMPLE
1. Antithetic: A vs. B	A. "There is nothing that goes into a person from the outside which can make him ritually unclean. B. Rather, it is what comes out of a person that makes him unclean." (Mk 7.15)
2. Synonymous: A = B	a. "Ask and you will receive; A. b1. seek, and you will find: b2. knock, and the door will be opened to you. a. "For everyone who asks will receive, B. b1. and everyone who seeks will find, b2. and the door will be opened to him who knocks." (Mt. 7.7-8)
3. Synthetic: A + B = C	A. "Happy are those who know they are spiritually poor: B. the kingdom of heaven belongs to them!" (Mt. 5.3) C. (the poor are saved)
4. Climactic: a B	a. "Whoever welcomes in my name one of these children, B. welcomes me; and a. whoever welcomes me, B. welcomes not only me but also the one who sent me." (Mk. 9.37)
5. Chiasmic: a b // B A	a. "Whoever exalts himself b. will be humbled, and B. whoever humbles himself A. will be exalted. (Mt. 23.12)

* Adapted from Stein, 1978, pp. 27-31; Burney, 1925.

The interesting chiasmic type--in this instance (Mt. 23.12) also antithetical--appears as:

a. Whoever exalts himself		A. will be exalted.
↓		↑
b. will be humbled, and	————	B. whoever humbles himself

The same can be done with the sayings about losing one's life to save it (Mk. 8.35) and the last shall be first (Mk. 10.31 or Mt. 20.16). As for the synthetic example (Mt. 5.3), which constitutes the first of the "Beatitudes," textually it belongs with the third Beatitude (v.5), together forming a stanza with two couplets in synonymous parallelism, each couplet having two lines in synthetic parallelism (Black, 1967, p. 156):

A.
  a. Blessed are God's poor,
  b. for theirs is the Kingdom of heaven.

B.
  a. Blessed are God's humble,
  b. for they inherit the earth.

A similar point can be made about the example of synonymous parallelism, where synonymity is observed within each clause, among the clauses in each sentence, and between the two sentences. At a still more encompassing level, Manson (1935, pp. 54-56) has identified a dozen and more instances of parallelism of whole strophes. For example, in the sayings about cares (Lk. 12), the saying about the wild flowers ("lilies of the field") in verses 27-28 parallels the previous saying about the crows ("birds of the air") in verse 24. Of course, we must reserve the possibility that these utterances or passages were paired by the oral and written tradition rather than by Jesus; yet in some cases they can easily be imagined to have been spoken together.

All of these examples also reveal an element of rhythm which seems to follow from the parallelism and repetition (as C. F. Burney first pointed out). Moreover, Robert Tannehill (1975, pp. 46-51) has identified a special kind of rhythm in several parallel sayings, a recurrence of sense and syntactical units. Although his analysis is based on the Greek text, the rhythm can emerge in the English as well. For instance, one need only read aloud the synonymous example in Table 8 to discern this syntactical rhythm. That example was just used here to illustrate parallelism at various levels within an utterance. In this case the repeated recurrence of multiple parallel units of similar syntax and length as well as of meaning makes it impossible not to feel the rhythm. Tannehill also notes an instance of a parable in antithetical parallelism (Mt. 7.24-27), where rhythm is discerned in the consistent pattern of word-order and in the similarity of meaning and of length of clauses. Thus the parallel structure of many of Jesus' sayings brings with it a distinct rhythm by means of recurrent patterns of meaning, syntax, and length within units of words, clauses, sentences, couplets, and perhaps even strophes.

We conclude that the structure of Jesus' sayings is characterized by the parallelism of members. He spoke especially in antitheses, with an unusual stress on the second part of what he was saying, such that it was the second part that countered the first. Thus we find the distinctiveness of his teaching embodied not only in antitheses but also in the distinctive way in which he laid stress on the second part of his sayings as an antithesis to the first part. This structural feature moreover befits the general style and content of Jesus' teaching--authoritative and original--epitomized in his whole manner of presentation (e.g., Mt. 5.43-44):

A. You have heard it said ...

B. But now I tell you ...!

That too is antithetical parallelism, and that too lays unmistakable stress on the second line--it is Antithesis writ large.

* * * * *

Let us combine the findings so far to suggest a thematic conclusion regarding Jesus' language. We have found that the sayings of Jesus are characterized by a particular quality of sound and structure.

(a) The repetition of vowels and consonants, and the repetition of near words (as in puns) combine in such a way as to express, in different ways appropriate to different purposes, a juxtaposition of terms or images given modulated form in a congruent juxtaposition of sounds.

(b) The different rhythms each carry a distinctive mood or character in such a way as to befit the different content and purpose of the saying being delivered.

(c) The antithetical structure gives form to the antithesis in the content of the sayings and it gives stress to the distinctive opposition embodied in the message and manner of the teacher who is presenting the antithesis and who is representing an antithesis.

To this point it must be evident that Jesus' language is pedagogically accomplished as well as rhetorically fine. It did not merely deliver his message but *befitted his teaching*: the sound and structure are congruent with the image and content of the saying, with the purpose and audience of its expression, and with the manner and meaning of the teacher who was speaking it.

Scholars have studied Jesus' sayings now for paronomasia, now for rhythm, now for parallelism; each effort has revealed for that particular linguistic feature a degree of congruence with the content or purpose of a saying;--can the sayings now be examined for several linguistic features at once? We note, for example:

(a) instances of paronomasia cited by Black that are also cited by Jeremias as instances of 4-beat rhythm (Mk. 9.50), of antithetical parallelism (Mk. 4.4-8, 31-32), and specifically of antithesis by opposition-cum-negation (Mt. 6.19) and by polarization (Lk. 14. 8-10);

(b) instances of 4-beat rhythm which also instance antithesis by polarization (Mk. 4.25) and by complementarity (Mt. 16.19);

(c) an instance of antithesis by inversion which also instances 3+2-beat rhythm (Mk. 8.35);

(d) an instance of antithetical-chiasmic parallelism which also appears to represent paronomasia (Mt. 23.12);

(e) an instance of riddle, word-play, and probable antithesis (Mk. 9.31); and

(f) instances of 3+2-beat rhythm which also instance rhyme and word-play and antithesis (Mt. 11.17, 20.16).

These dozen examples may represent isolated instances. A careful examination of the texts on the part of an Aramaic scholar with an interest in rhetorical form, and with an eye to discern the several forms in any one saying, might yield fruitful findings. Jesus' language may well prove even more rhetorically and pedagogically accomplished than we have come to appreciate, however highly, up to now.

The Forms

Under the rubric of form we will review five categories of Jesus' language: his figures of speech, parables, illustrations, dialectic, and discourse. Although some of these may have significant theological implications, our interest in them remains from an educational perspective.

Figures of speech

One of the most striking aspects of Jesus' language is his sayings, particularly their pith and turn of phrase. The range of figures is in itself impressive. Table 9 lists 17 figures of speech together with one example of each.

A glance at Table 9 reveals the range and variety of Jesus' figures of speech. In Stein's (1978) comprehensive listing, approximately 225 instances are cited for the 10 figures specified--20 for overstatement, 30 for paradox, 50 and 60 for metaphor and proverb (pp. 8-22). To be sure, the terms and

Table 9. Jesus' Figures of Speech*

	FIGURE	EXAMPLE
1.	overstatement	"So if your hand makes you lose you faith, cut it off!" (Mk 9.43ff.)
2.	hyperbole	"It is much harder for a rich person to enter the Kingdom of God than for a camel to go through the eye of a needle" (Mk 10.25).
3.	pun	You strain a galma/fly out of your drink, but swallow a gamla/camel!" (Mt. 23.24).
4.	simile	"I am sending you out just like sheep to a pack of wolves" (Mt. 10.16).
5.	metaphor	"Be on your guard against the yeast of the Pharisees and the yeast of Herod" (Mk. 8.15).
6.	proverb	"For your heart will always be where your riches are" (Mt. 6.21).
7.	riddle	"From the time John preached his message until this very day the Kingdom of Heaven has suffered violent attacks, and violent men try to seize it" (Mt. 11.12).
8.	paradox	"If one of you wants to be great, he must be the servant of the rest" (Mk 10.43).
9.	irony	"You can predict the weather by looking at the sky, but you cannot interpret the signs concerning these times!" (Mt. 16.3)
10.	synecdoche	"I have food to eat that you know nothing about" (Jn 4.32).
11.	metonymy	"I did not come to bring peace, but a sword" (Mt. 10.34).
12.	personification	"The wind blows wherever it wishes" (Jn. 3.8).
13.	apostrophe	"Jerusalem, Jerusalem! You kill the prophets and stone the messengers God has sent you! (Mt. 23.37)
14.	allusion	"Tear down this Temple, and in three days I will build it again" (Jn. 2.19).
15.	allegory	"I am the vine, and you are the branches" (Jn. 15.5).
16.	pregnant comparison	"They are blind leaders of the blind; and when one blind man leads another, both fall into a ditch" (Mt. 15.14).
17.	epigram	"For whoever wants to save his own life will lose it; but whoever loses his life for me and for the gospel will save it. Does a person gain anything if he wins the whole world but loses his life?" (Mt. 8.35-36).

*selected from Griffith-Jones, 1914; Horne, 1920, Rixon, 1977; Stein, 1978.

definitions for the different types in Table 9 may vary. Moreover, we must bear in mind that many of the sayings attributed to Jesus may derive from Christian tradition rather than word-for-word from Jesus. Yet these considerations do not to any appreciable extent diminish the impression that here is a speaker who could phrase a large number of sayings in a wide variety of ways, any one of them well turned-out. Plurality, range, and variety overall--in addition to singular distinction individually--are characteristic of Jesus' figures of speech.

Parables

A major part of Jesus' language is in parabolic form. The gospels make it a point that "he used parables to teach them many things" (e.g., Mk. 4.1; cf. Lk. 18.1). Our interest here is restricted to the language form of parables in relation to his teaching. (On his parables more generally see the authoritative study by Jeremias, 1963, and other studies reviewed in Perrin, 1976.)

The first thing to note is that Jesus' parables are not merely characteristic but distinctive of his teaching. To be sure, parables had long been told by many other teachers in several traditions, including the rabbinical schools of Jesus' day. But Jesus' parables are unique to him. "We find nothing to be compared with the parables of Jesus" (Jeremias, 1971, p. 29). They are not fables, they are not allegories, they are not phantasies; they are neither aloof nor complicated nor allusive nor expansive. To the contrary:

> Their nearness to life, their simplicity and clarity, the masterly brevity with which they are told, the seriousness of their appeal to the conscience, their loving understanding of the outcasts of religion--all this is without analogy. (p. 30)

From a rhetorical point of view (Wilder, 1971) the parables of Jesus are not stereotypic, formulaic, or rigid as in other traditions; they are marked by the immediacy and presence of the speaker and the direct personal appeal or challenge to the hearer (pp. 77, 82). Finally, an essential difference is that other teachers would tell an occasional parable in order to illustrate some statement or to prove some point which they had just made, whereas Jesus habitually spoke parables as the very content of his teaching (Schweizer, 1971, p. 27).

For various reasons a precise definition of parable is not easy to agree on. It is in the nature of a figure of speech, much like a metaphor or a simile, in that a parable likens one (unknown) thing to another (known). A wide range of speech forms are called methal (parable) in the ancient Aramaic tradition. Jeremias (1971, p. 30) counts 41 parables in the synoptic gospels. Yet another problem is that some parables appear not to have come from Jesus but from the Christian tradition. Applying the very strictest of critical standards, Perrin (1967, 1976, p. 41) emphasized that scholars recognize as authentic at least the 22 parables listed in Table 10.

Table 10 arranges the parables by shorter, example-like types and longer, story-like ones. This otherwise unimportant division serves only to remind that Jesus' parables are by no means necessarily "stories," although a good half of them are. Since the story-like ones may be more familiar, some of the shorter type will be quoted as examples. We recall that the central theme of Jesus' message was "the Kingdom of God" (Mk. 1.15). Here is how Jesus taught that message in form of parable. "The Kingdom of God is like this," says Jesus:

(a) A woman takes some yeast and mixes it with a bushel of flour until the whole batch of dough rises. (Lk. 13.21)

(b) A man is looking for fine pearls, and when he finds one that is unusually fine, he goes and sells everything he has, and buys that pearl. (Mt. 13.45-46)

(c) A man takes a mustard seed, the smallest seed in the world, and plants it in the ground. After a while it grows up and becomes the biggest of all plants. It puts out such large branches that the birds come and make their nests in its shade. (Mk. 4.31-32)

Table 10. Jesus' Use of Parables*

	SHORTER, EXAMPLE-LIKE		LONGER, STORY-LIKE
1.	Growing seed - Mk 4.26-29	1.	Sower - Mk. 4.3-8
2.	Mustard seed - Mk 4.30-32	2.	Vineyard tenants - Mk 12.1-12
3.	Children playing - Mt. 11.16-19	3.	Unforgiving servant - Mt. 18.23-35
4.	Hidden treasure - Mt. 13.44	4.	Vineyard workers - Mt. 20.1-6
5.	Pearl - Mt. 13.45-46	5.	Two sons - Mt. 21.28-32
6.	Friend at midnight - Lk 11.5-8	6.	Good Samaritan - Lk. 10.29-37
7.	Yeast - Lk. 13.20-21	7.	Great feast - Lk 14.16-24
8.	Tower builder - Lk 14.28-30	8.	Lost son - Lk. 15.11-32
9.	Warring king - Lk. 14.31-32	9.	Shrewd manager - Lk. 16.1-9
10.	Lost sheep - Lk 15.3-7	10.	Widow & judge - Lk 18.1-8
11.	Lost coin - Lk. 15.8-9	11.	Pharisee & tax-collector - Lk 18.9-14

*arrangement of Perrin's (1976, p. 41) list of 'authentic' parables

And, too, the Kingdom of God is like a friendly foreigner, a great feast, a shrewd manager--the story-parables in Lk. 10.29-37, 14.16-24, 16.1-9. Nothing could be simpler, but what does it mean?

Ever since Jesus first uttered these short similitudes, whole volumes of interpretation have been written on his few sentences. But Jesus' parables, no less than other forms of his teaching language, do not carry an intellectual message: they do not instruct in some "point"; they do not illustrate some proposition; they do not call for analysis and explanation but for decision and action.

When one reads through the parables in Table 10, the remarkable fact emerges that Jesus does not specify their point. As Eduard Schweizer (1971) among others has correctly noted, Jesus does not even put into words the "statement" which the parable supposedly leads to.

> Jesus is therefore not simply a good school teacher who adapts himself to the limited intellectual capacity of his pupils by using metaphors and illustrations so as to drum a rather difficult proposition into their heads better. (p. 27)

Similarly, Wilder (1971) stresses that Jesus' parables are "action-images" (p. 84).

> We speak of Jesus' vivid parables and his skill in teaching. This is not to say enough. Jesus is not merely clarifying difficult ideas. He is leading men to make a judgment and to come to a decision. (pp. 74-75)

Explanation or interpretation are not necessary and moreover are not befitting, for the parables do not give out instruction or take to cognition. If in spite of its surpassing clarity a parable is not clear, then another parable will be told. This nice point is made by Edward Schillebeeckx (1979, p. 158):

> What may clarify the meaning of a parable is not argument but, if anything, the telling of a second or third parable--through the recurrently paradoxical effects of shock and 'estrangement' regarding our normal, everyday, conformist behavior.

But what shall we make, then, of those many parables whose concluding sentence in the gospel text forthrightly states the point? The researches of Joachim Jeremias (1963) have demonstrated that many of these conclusions plainly were appended to Jesus' parables by the early Christian tradition (e.g., Mk. 4.22, 25, 13.37; Mt. 20.16, 21.44, 22.14, 25.13, 29; Lk. 5.39, 11.10, 12.21, 48b, 13.30, 16.10, 18.14b).

Few of these findings from historical, linguistic, rhetorical, and theological studies have made their way into the educational literature on Jesus' teaching. To the contrary, education writers typically regard Jesus' parables as illustrations mere. As illustrations, they are useful for the purpose of instructing simple-minded folk (e.g., Rixon, 1977; Wilson, 1975) and they serve to illuminate the didactic point or concept which Jesus had previously introduced in a lecture (Roberts, 1955; Squires, 1927). The point is then again made as the conclusion to the parable, witness Mt. 20.16 and 22.14 (Ibid.) [cf. these two verses in Jeremias' list of appended conclusions, *supra*]. In imitation of Jesus' parabolic method, modern teachers are urged first to state the analogy, then to describe its details, and last to state the conclusion; if the parable still remains unclear to students, the patient teacher must "explain and elucidate its details further" (Colman, 1967, p. 49).

Such views may derive from the stress on intellect which some educators discover in the teaching of Jesus. For example, Squires (1927) repeatedly emphasizes that the imparting of facts about religion "was evidently one of his chief objectives" (p. 239). "Jesus taught his pupils to think deeply, clearly, and accurately. His methods indicate that he placed a high estimate on the value of intellectual nurture" (p. 137). Of the parables McKoy (1930) concludes that "it was the evident purpose of the Master to provoke thought on the part of his followers"--witness Jesus' withholding their key and the many subsequent books written to interpret them (p. 47).

It is ironic that these viewpoints from education should miss altogether the nature and pedagogic function of parables in Jesus' teaching. Educators emphasize precisely those aspects which do not characterize Jesus' parables, and whose very absence serves to distinguish his parables from all others. Jesus' parables are a form of teaching but not instruction; they embody a message but do not illustrate a proposition; they deliver content but do not transmit knowledge; they require understanding but not intellect; they call for a response in action and attitude, not in mentation and analysis. They are clear enough for the purpose, save when stalled by explaining away.

Illustrations

Jesus' language is full of imagery. Just as he would tell a parable rather than utter a proposition, so Jesus would speak illustrations rather than explanations. This feature is but one aspect of Jesus' more general manner of expressing his teaching in non-intellectual form. As many scholars have noted, such as C. H. Dodd (1970), Jesus speaks in pictures rather than propositions (p. 39). Instead of saying "Charity should not be ostentatious," he says something like, When you give money, don't make a big show of it (Mt. 6.2). Instead of enunciating some abstract principle about the comparative importance of interpersonal relations and religious obligations, Jesus pictures a man going up to an altar and suddenly remembering a grudge that someone has against him--Leave the altar, Jesus says, first go make peace with your neighbor, and only then come back to make your offering (Mt. 5.23-24).

Much that Jesus says in a teaching way is an illustration; and the illustrations depict the range and variety of human life. Table 11 gives an extensive list.

Table 11 serves to impress upon us a point which is not noticed about Jesus' illustrations. Most authors remark on their simple, everyday, down-to-earth content about homelife and nature, especially pastoral and agricultural--the birds of the air, the sheep, the harvest and so forth (e.g., Squires, 1927). While that is true, Table 11 also details categories of illustrations about commerce, finance, law, government, warfare, construction. Of the 230 instances cited by Griffith-Jones (1914), only 36 fit under the "home &

Table 11. Jesus' Use of Illustrations*

HOME	NATURE					
<u>Family events & problems</u>	<u>Animals</u>	<u>Birds</u>	<u>Other</u>	<u>Plants/Trees</u>		<u>Human body</u>
weddings, marriage, funeral	dogs	vultures	moth	lilies	sycamore	eye
bridegroom, widow	swine	ravens	gnat	reed	mustard	ear
parents, children	oxen	eagles	viper	grass	fig	hands
sons working for fathers	ass	doves	scorpion	thorns	olive	feet
debt, burglars	foxes	sparrows	serpents	mint		cheek
	sheep	hen	fish	anise		blood
<u>Domestic chores</u>	goats	chicks		cumin		
	camel	cock				
care of clothing & linen	wolves	nests				
moth damage						
sweeping floor						
straightening a room						
maintaining the lighting						

<u>Catering</u>	<u>Agriculture</u>	<u>Vinticulture</u>	<u>Weather</u>
lighting a fire	plowing	hedging vineyard	lightning
cooking fish	sowing	pruning vines	wind
price of sparrows	kinds of soil	pruning dead branches	sun
use of salt	growing wheat - seed, blade,	pressing grapes	rain
shortage of food	ear, corn	fruits & trees	red sky threatening
making bread -	harvesting -	laborers & managers	clouds rising
grinding grain,	separating tares		earthquake
adding leaven, heating	burning tares		fire
oven	gathering into barn		storm
washing dishes			heat
giving feast, meal			floods
eggs, bread, wine,			
water,			
fruit, fish			

Table 11. Illustrations (continued)

WORK & BUSINESS	SOCIAL RELATIONS	GOVERNMENT	NATIONAL TRADITIONS
hiring laborers	family	law	The Law
trading in pearls	friends	suits	The Temple
lending money	enemies	judge	synagogue
banking	thieves	judgement	prophets
creditor, debtor	robbers	testimony	Scriptures
steward, servants	dissipation	witness	religious sects, ritual,
buying land, oxen	drunkenness	hearing	practices
trading with talents	outcasts	evidence	etc.
making yokes	rich & poor	war	
building barns	insane, sick	armies	
constructing tower	charity, gifts, etc.	trenches	
laying foundation		swords	
squandering property	**HUMAN ACTIVITY**	taxes	
misuse of wealth		tax collectors	
unemployment	birth	Emperor	
devouring widows'	sleep	King	
houses	death	Prince	
tailoring	eating		
sheepherding, fishing	drinking		
costing out a building	laughing		
project	weeping		
	mourning		
	etc.		

*adapted from Griffith-Jones, 1914; Rixon, 1977; Ross 1904.

household" category and only 31 under "pastoral & agricultural life"--not even one-third (29%) of the total. Jesus' illustrations cannot be regarded as applying only, or even predominantly, to the simple, everyday, peasant world. They encompass a world of people and activity. Plurality, range, and variety characterize Jesus' illustrations.

Dialectic

Jesus' teaching activity was occupied with impressing upon people the urgency of his message. A large part of what he said--perhaps the greater part--was directed to people who did not share his sense of urgency and who remained unwitting, indifferent or otherwise ill-disposed, even hostile, to his message and activity. Hence we find that much of his language takes on the forceful forms of argument, disputation, and vituperation.

(1) *Argument*

Many of Jesus' sayings take on the form of argument. Stein (1978, pp. 20-21) cites 12 examples for *a fortiori* alone. Table 12 lists seven types of argument together with one example for each.

We surely cannot characterize Jesus' language as argumentative, still less as couched in classical logic. Yet Jesus certainly pressed his case and at times had to defend it. We can appreciate that a good portion of his utterances will have assumed the form of argument.

(2) *Disputation*

As the gospel texts make clear, often in a vivid and dramatic way, Jesus frequently engaged in disputations with religious officials over his views on law, doctrine, and practice. He showed remarkable skill in handling objections and confounding opponents, particularly by his use of *counter-questions*.

The synoptics record 17 instances in which Jesus responded to a polemical stimulus with a question (Dillon, 1981b). For example:

Table 12. Jesus' Use of Argument*

ARGUMENT	EXAMPLE
1. analogy	"If one of you is planning to build a tower, he sits down first and figures out what it will cost, ... In the same way, none of you can be my disciple unless he gives up everything he has" (Lk. 14.28-33).
2. dilemma	"What does our Law allow us to do on the Sabbath? To help or to harm? To save a man's life or to destroy it? (Mk. 3.4)
3. reductio ad absurdum	"How can Satan drive out Satan? If a country divides itself into groups which fight each other, that country will fall apart. ...So if Satan's kingdom divides into groups, it cannot last, but will fall apart and come to an end" (Mk. 3.23-26).
4. argumentum ad hominem	"Whichever of you has committed no sin may throw the first stone at her" (Jn. 8.7).
5. argumentum a fortiori	"As bad as you are, you know how to give good things to your children. How much more, then, will your Father in heaven give good things to those who ask him!" (Mt. 7.11)
6. tu quoque a fortiori	"Moses ordered you to circumcise your sons, and so you circumcise a boy on the Sabbath. If a boy is circumcised on the Sabbath so that Moses' Law is not broken, why are you angry with me because I made a man completely well on the Sabbath?" (Jn. 7.22-23)
7. argumentum ex concessu	"Is it easier to say to this paralyzed man, 'Your sins are forgiven', or to say, 'Get up, pick up your mat, and walk'? I will prove to you, then, that the Son of Man has authority on earth to forgive sins. I tell you, get up, pick up your mat, and go home!" (Mk. 2.9-11)

*selected from Curtis, 1943 (cf. Rixon, 1977); Montague, 1884; Stein, 1978.

> Why do your disciples disobey the teaching handed down by our ancestors?
>
> -- And why do you disobey God's command and follow your own teaching? (Mt. 15.2-3)

In 9 of the 12 disputations recorded, Jesus replied not with an answer but with a counter-question (Mk. 2.1-2, 18-20, 23-38, 3.1-5, 22-26, 10.2-9, 11.27-33, 12.13-17; Lk. 7.36-47). By his counter-question Jesus re-defined the issue, turned the tables, and required his opponents to answer on his own terms. In one case they refused to answer, and so did he, and there the dispute ended with the frustration of the opponents' question.

Question[1]	What right do you have to do these things? Who gave you such right?
Question[2]	-- I will ask you just one question, and if you give me an answer, I will tell you what right I have to do these things. Tell me, where did John's right to baptize come from: was it from God or from man?
Refusal [2]	... We don't know.
Refusal [1]	-- Neither will I tell you, then, by what right I do these things. (Mk. 11.28-33)

By contrast, Jesus always replied with an *answer* in pedagogical exchanges--that is, in non-disputations. Of 18 pedagogical exchanges, Jesus replied with a question in only 6 cases and in all cases he went on to give the answer (Mk. 6.35-38, 8.2-6, 9.11-13, 28, 10.26-27; Lk. 10.29-37, 13.23-24, 17.20-21, 21.7-8; Mt. 11.2-6, 13.10, 18.1-5, 21-22, 19.27-28, 21.20-21). We may therefore say that Jesus' language in disputation is characterized by the use of an interrogative rather than declarative form, the counter-question.

(3) *Vituperation*

This is a feature of Jesus' language which seems insufficiently appreciated, or least remarked on. (Alone among education writers, B. A. Hinsdale [1895] stands out for his noting this aspect, even devoting a chapter to Jesus' "severity.") Although not a major part of his total speech, Jesus' use of vituperative language is a rhetorical accomplishment on the grand scale.

Consider first the awful names which Jesus called people, that is, his name-calling: Hypocrites! Blind fools! Descendants of murderers! You snakes and sons of snakes! (Mt. 23. 17, 25, 31, 33) Then there are his aspersions, such as this inventive one:

> You hypocrites! You are like whitewashed tombs, which look fine on the outside but are full of bones and decaying corpses on the inside. (Mt. 23.27)

What a terrible thing to say about somebody; Jesus said it *to* somebody. Another one of his ripostes to religious purists carried terrific invective, for the purists were considered to be the elect whereas the others named were specifically excluded from salvation:

> I tell you, the tax collectors and the prostitutes are going into the Kingdom of God ahead of you. (Mt. 21.31)

To a town which rejected him, Jesus hurls out:

> And as for you, Capernaum! Did you want to lift yourself up to heaven? You will be thrown down to hell! (Lk. 10.15)

And if someone were to cause another to sin, threatens Jesus:

> It would be better for him if a large millstone were tied around his neck and he were thrown into the sea. (Lk. 17.2)

Referring to the Romans' massacre of Galilean 'agitators' in the act of worship--an event electrifying at the time--Jesus warns:

> And I tell you that if you do not turn from your sins, you will all die as they did. (Lk. 13.3)

Curses and insults, threats and menacings, death and damnation--this language is far removed from the lyric and pastorale so often cited as Jesus' way of speaking. Indeed, we can agree with Joseph Baird's (1969) analysis of Jesus' speech (toward opponents) as showing him to be a provocative, aggressive, and intensely critical person (p. 133). Hinsdale (1895) remarked that these "torrents of terrific denunciation" offer such a contrast to the Beatitudes that we either exclude them from view "or, if we do not forget the fact, we underestimate its importance" (pp. 201, 202). The result is "false ideas of the character of Jesus, both as a person and as a teacher" (p. 201).

The force and imaginativeness of Jesus' invective are also seen in the twists which Jesus gave to his accusations against religious officials. The priests turn a house of prayer into a hideout for thieves (Mk. 11.17). The theologians don't practice what they preach (Mt. 23.3), and though they hold the key to knowledge they lock its door against others while refusing to go in themselves (Lk. 11.52). The religionists (Pharisees, rabbis, theologians) scrupulously tithe even down to the smallest things like herbs but neglect the big things like justice (Mt. 23.23); they rob poor widows of their homes and then make a show of saying long prayers (Mk. 12.40). Other instances of vituperation are not hard to find (e.g., Mt. 23.4, 23, 23.37; Mk. 10.14; Lk. 10. 13-14, 18.15).

The few examples quoted show something of the variety of Jesus' vituperative language. The range of types can further be seen in the list cited by Jeremias (1971, p. 19) in connection with another purpose: attack, repudiation, rebuff, threat, warning, intimidation, reprimand, judgment, accusation (Mk. 7.8, 8.12, 10.18, 25; Mt. 7.24, 10.34, 11.18, 23, 23.23). Jesus says awful things: his vituperativeness is terrific, various, and creative. A significant proportion of Jesus' language consists of vituperation, and it is characterized by force, range, and inventiveness.

Discourse

The final aspect of form to be considered is the mode of discourse in which Jesus spoke as a teacher. We can say of Socrates, for example, that his language is characterized by questions and dialogues. What form of discourse characterizes Jesus' teaching language? Here we need only look under a new angle at the language we have already reviewed, such as the parables and sayings; sorting it into the broad categories of discursive and interactive language.

(1) *Discursive mode*

Under this category we may place Jesus' narrative-type parables and his "discourses." The discourses include the Sermon on the Mount (Mt. 5-7), the Olivet Discourse (Mt. 24-25), the Upper Room Discourse (Jn. 15-16), and perhaps the missionary instructions (Mt. 10) and warnings about the final days (Mk. 13). Although these occupy fully several chapters of the gospel texts, they are plainly enough not unitary oral deliverances but editorial collections of various utterances originally spoken separately on different occasions. We do not know how often and at what length Jesus might have delivered sermons, addresses, and the like. But he surely did speak in connected discourse, even if not in the expansive way depicted by the Sermon on the Mount.

The character of Jesus, his conduct and message, the urgency and occasionality of his teaching activity--these do not leave the impression that he could have spoken at much length. Perhaps the story parables represent the longer form of Jesus' discourse. Even these may not have formed part of an extended teaching episode before some crowd; Trocme (1973) concludes that "most of the parables were part of the conversation at meals in the houses where Jesus had been invited" (p. 91).

(2) *Interactive mode*

Here we may place the numerous conversations, dialogues or discussions in which Jesus took part. A great many of the gospel scenes depict circumstantial meetings, incidents, or situations which Jesus used as an occasion to teach. Other scenes appear to be more structured occasions, as when Jesus would be approached with a question or objection to answer. These latter scenes may be divided into two broad types, called "controversy and scholastic dialogues" by Rudolf Bultmann (1968), who identified a dozen of each type in the synoptic gospels. In our own study (Dillon, 1981b) we distinguish between 12 polemical and 18 pedagogical exchanges.

In addition to these scenes, education writers typically cite discussions and conversations in the gospel of John. Jesus engages in discussions with the people in the synagogue at Capernaum (Jn. 6.25-59) and with the disciples in the Upper Room just before his arrest (Jn. 13.21-14.31). He engages in conversations with Nicodemus (Jn. 3.1-21) and with a Samaritan woman (Jn. 4.5-26). The last scene above all others is cited as paradigmatic of Jesus' teaching approach and indeed as a model of teaching (e.g., Hinsdale, 1895; Horne, 1920; Price, 1946; Roberts, 1955). These scenes in John give particular evidence of having been composed to fit a series of Jesus' sayings selected by the evangelist. Nonetheless the general point remains that a good part of Jesus' teaching was spoken in the interactive modes of conversation and discussion.

Under the interactive category we may also place Jesus' questions, of which we find some 100 in the synoptic gospels (Dillon, 1981b). About 40% of his questions fit into our previous category, in that they appear in the midst of some discourse, and for that fact may be considered rhetorical questions. Of the remaining 60% which occur in interactions, most are either counter-questions or mere conversational replies--that is, Jesus does not initiate but reacts with a question. One is indeed struck by the relatively few questions which Jesus posed for people to answer, and the even fewer which seem to serve a pedagogical function--perhaps only nine in all can be counted (Mk. 8.19, 20; Lk. 7.42, 10.36; Mt. 13.51, 17.25, 21.31; and of doubtful authenticity, Mk. 8.27,29).

In sum, we find that Jesus' teaching language is not characterized by any one particular form of discourse, such as one can say that the interrogative and dialogical form characterizes Socrates' discourse. Rather, Jesus' pedagogical language is positively characterized by a variety of forms of discourse.

* * * *

We are left with the general impression that Jesus' language contains a plurality of instances of speech covering a range and variety of types within several categories of form (e.g., types within the category of figures of speech). Not one but many forms characterize Jesus' language.

Rhetorical Qualities

The rhetorical qualities of Jesus' language may seem evident. But how to describe this quality is not as evident and it remains to some extent a matter of selection and emphasis. Here we will evaluate Jesus' *style*, that is, that aspect of rhetoric which refers to a speaker's *way of saying* what it is that he has to say (see Winterowd, 1975).

We first distinguish between characteristic and distinctive elements of Jesus' style. Then we select for special emphasis the style in which he addressed people. Last we assess the relations between his language and other aspects of his teaching. These four qualities are variety, originality, immediacy, and congruence.

Variety

What is Jesus' characteristic (but not also distinctive) way of speaking? No single feature seems salient enough to satisfy that question, but we can identify several features that are characteristic. The speaker characteristically phrases what he says in paronomasia, alliteration, and assonance; in rhythm and rhyme; in antithetical parallelisms; in various modes of discourse, various types of argument and vituperation, and in a range of figures of speech, illustrations, and parables.

Although "poetic" is one of the terms most frequently used, the term does not encompass this language, nor does it befit parts of it. Surely Jesus' language has aspects which can be described as poetic. Thus Burney (1925) entitled his work *The Poetry of Our Lord.* Yet to characterize his language as poetic seems inadequate. For example, Rixon (1977) speaks of Jesus "wrapping up His teaching in such a pictorial, poetic and portable form" (p. 54). He wrapped his teaching up in other forms too, also characteristic. Manson (1935) regarded the stophic parallelism of Jesus' sayings "as the most distinctive characteristic of his poetry and his special contribution to the forms of poetry in general" (p. 56). Whatever the case with strophes, the most distinctive characteristic of his parallelisms is their secondary stress, while parallelism is not distinctive, albeit characteristic, of Jesus. McKoy (1930) characterized Jesus as not only an artist of teaching "but, in particular, a poet. Jesus had the poet's vision, the poet's imagination, the poet's spontaneity, and the poet's sympathy" (p. 115). That is to exaggerate selected features to make of Jesus, as the cited heading does indeed make of him, "Jesus a Poet." Finally, it seems an exaggeration to assert with Curtis (1943, p. 74):

> It is indeed no exaggeration to assert that it was His idiom, natural or deliberate, to preach and teach in the form of poetry. ... He spoke in poetry, and He should be interpreted as a poet.

We know that he could not have presented himself to contemporaries as a poet; he was interpreted as a teacher, a prophet, a blasphemer, a doer of good and evil--but for certain no contemporary, friend or foe, ever interpreted Jesus as a poet.

Only some part of Jesus' language has poetic features, and in essential respects even that one part is doubtfully poetic. Jesus' parables have been characterized as "a superlative work of art" and his epigrams as "literary gems of the rarest beauty" (McKoy, 1930, pp. 42, 159). But we can agree with Tannehill's (1975) analysis that, while some of his sayings have features akin to poetry, they are not aesthetic objects and do not invite aesthetic enjoyment. To the contrary, they disinvite contemplation and enjoyment and they demand decision and action. "It is especially this strong appeal to the will which distinguishes these sayings from aesthetic objects" (p. 17). Imaginative force follows from the pattern and tension in many of Jesus' sayings: pattern refers to features of parallelism, repetition, and rhythm; tension refers to antithesis, metaphor, and extremeness of language (pp. 39-57). Some of these are the very features which have lead to the characterization of Jesus' language as poetry. Yet the characterization skews these features while ignoring other, more central, features and while ignoring other, equally characteristic, portions of his language apart from his sayings.

Thus to characterize it as poetry would appear to make Jesus' language not his own. It deroutes our understanding of the way he spoke and acted as a teacher; it dismisses the expressed content of his teaching; and it renders incomprehensible the extreme reactions which people gave to him when he taught. It was not with a laurel that people crowned Jesus, whether when executing or elevating him.

The less colorful but more encompassing terms of plurality, range, and variety assess Jesus' characteristic speech by taking note of the frequency of utterances of different types within several categories. That surely betokens a command of language, an ability to manipulate its sounds, structure, and forms. Hence we may evaluate Jesus' characteristic way of speaking as mastery of language.

Originality

A speaker's originality is revealed by his distinctiveness or novelty within a given linguistic context. Some aspects of Jesus' language stand out against the language of his tradition and his contemporaries. We will call "original" six features which both characterize and distinguish Jesus' way of speaking when compared with traditional and contemporary language of his day. The first three features are original in some or many respects, whereas the last three are wholly original with Jesus.

(1) *Parallelisms*

What distinguishes Jesus' use of antithetical parallelisms is the range or versatility of contexts and the stress on the second part of the saying. In the Old Testament and then-contemporary usage of parallelisms, the context is restricted and the stress is uniformly on the first part (Jeremias, 1971, pp. 18-19).

(2) *Riddles*

The form of riddle is not original with Jesus but its use in teaching was. A dozen and more riddles may be found in Jesus' sayings, whereas teachers at the time did not use riddles (pp. 30-31).

(3) *Parables*

Nearly everything about Jesus' parables, save for the parabolic form itself, is unique to him. Features which are characteristic of traditional and contemporary parables are absent from Jesus' parables, and vice-versa. The realism of Jesus' parables, their simplicity, clarity, and brevity are all without analogy in the Judaic literature (pp. 29-30). Also *sui generis* to Jesus' parables is the way in which deep and lofty dimensions of mystery and divinity "are married to such ordinariness and secularity" (Wilder, 1971, p. 76). Moreover, Jesus used parables to embody the very content of his teaching rather than, as was customary, to illustrate or to prove some didactic point previously made (Schweizer, 1971, p. 27).

(4) *Kingdom* [reign] *of God*

Some five dozen times in the synoptic gospels, for a familiar example in the Lord's Prayer (Lk. 11.2), Jesus speaks of the reign of God, *malkuta*, and its coming (Jeremias, 1971, pp. 31-33). This way of speaking is without analogy in the Judaic literature and it has no parallel in the language of Jesus' contemporaries--in the terms and phrases, their usage, content, and their centrality as a theme of teaching.

> What must be set down as the original work of Jesus is that he made the rarely used term *malkuta* the central concept of his public preaching. With this word he associated such a wealth of otherwise uninstanced phrases, that we

> must regard these linguistic creations as a characteristic of his way of speaking. (p. 103)

These numerous innovative features betoken Jesus' "power to create new eschatological language" (p. 34). "He created his own terminology" (Dalman, 1902, p. 136). "It was not merely the content of the conception which forms the kernel of our Lord's teaching that was new and original, but also His application of the term" (p. 139). Thus here we find originality at the very core of Jesus' teaching, original in message as well as in language.

(5) *'amen*

"The mode in which Jesus used *'amen* is unfamiliar to the entire range of Jewish literature" (Dalman, 1902, p. 226). In three dozen places in the synoptic gospels (e.g., Mk. 10.15) the word *'amen* is used by Jesus--and only by Jesus--together with the phrase "I tell you," to introduce his teaching (Jeremias, 1971, p. 35). In Jewish literature and practice, *'amen* was used without exception--as it still is today, both in Judaism and in Christianity--*after* a saying and as an assent to the words of *another*. The fact that the Aramaic word *'amen* is retained in the Greek gospels; the fact that it is never given in prefatory form otherwise than for Jesus; and the fact that the Christian tradition cited but did not imitate this usage;--these facts impress upon us how distinctly this way of speaking was perceived at the time to be new and unusual and peculiar to Jesus alone. "Here we have the creation of a new expression by Jesus" (p. 36).

This feature reveals a further aspect of originality in that beyond novelty it denotes uniqueness of origin. As Jesus used it to preface his sayings, *'amen* was perceived to signify an assertion of authority not only for the content of the subsequent words but also for their origin in the speaker himself--their *author*ity. Everybody else used *'amen* at the end to assent to someone else's words; every other teacher began by saying "It is written" or "Thus saith the Lord." By stark contrast Jesus began with: "Now I'm telling you for certain: --" ("Amen, I say unto you"). Thus Jesus' use of *'amen* was original and authoritative; moreover, it was clearly recognized as such by those who heard him speak.

It is useful to stress that we are describing merely the fact that Jesus' use of the prefacing *'amen* was original and was recognized at the time to be original. That is not to say that his auditors concurred in his usage. Its reversal of common usage made it striking to everyone. But to many who heard Jesus speak in this "original" way, it was also shocking and disturbing.

(6) *'abba*

This is one word which Jesus used for God, and the Greek gospels give it in Aramaic (Mk. 14.36). Jeremias identifies it as "the most important linguistic innovation on the part of Jesus" (1971, p. 36). Moreover, it is a significant part of Jesus' teaching and this way of speaking was immediately taken up by the Christian tradition (Rom. 8.15; Gal. 4.6). Jesus' originality in this case is particularly difficult for us to apperceive. As before, we have to learn the unfamiliar context in which he spoke; here we must also unlearn the familiar context in which we speak. Let us put it (inexactly) that no one in Jesus' time or before ever called God *'abba* but that nearly everyone since now calls God *'abba*. Hence to appreciate this original feature of Jesus' language we must perceive familiar usage as unfamiliar.

What does *'abba* mean? Better, what did it mean? In the first place *'abba* is an Aramaic address for one's father, so it means "my father." The world is now accustomed to modes of language and thought for God-as-personal-father, and so we see nothing remarkable in that. (Everyone is *accustomed*, not everyone is agreed.) But in Jesus' time and in his tradition--the language, the culture, the literature--it was not customary to speak or think of God as father. To the contrary, as we learn from Jeremias, "Jews deliberately avoided applying the word *'abba* to God" (p. 65). Hence Jesus' language was unusual in speaking (and thus conceiving) of God as father, and especially original in using the particular word *'abba* for God-as-father.

The word was common but this usage was unique. From his search of the sources Jeremias emphatically concluded: "*We do not have a single example* of God being addressed as *'Abba* in Judaism, but Jesus *always* addressed God in this way in his prayers" (p. 66). Dalman noted the implication. "The usage of family life is transferred to God: it is the language of the child to its father" (1902, p. 192). The word does not quite mean "father" as in a generic term for male parent-father but is a form of address which only children (younger or grownup) would use in speaking to their father, and by extension to respected elders. Thus it is a colloquial, everyday, personal, and childlike word for one's father. Perhaps we go too far to think of it as "Papa" or "Dad," but these terms deliver some of the sense and force, thereby helping us to appreciate how unseemly *'abba* was for God. "It would have seemed disrespectful, indeed unthinkable, to the sensibilities of Jesus' contemporaries to address God with this familiar word" (Jeremias, 1971, p. 67).

As before, we stress here only that Jesus' language was original and recognized by contemporaries to be such. Today many people take comfort in the "Our Father" as taught by Jesus. But many people at the time felt that it was not right to speak about God that way. They had reason to be offended by Jesus' "original" way of speaking.

We have seen that Jesus' habitual way of speaking has both characteristic and distinctive elements. The characteristic element is variety of language. The distinctive element is originality.

Immediacy

Immediacy refers to the act of speaking. It turns our attention away from the more static qualities of language and brings us to consider its dynamics. We now have language in the act of being spoken by a speaker to a hearer. Jesus' way of speaking to someone is marked by *immediacy*. That quality denotes not just the aspect of here-and-now but particularly Jesus' direct, personal, and urgent address to the person in face of him.

In his study of *Early Christian Rhetoric*, Amos Wilder (1971) raises the theme of immediacy by stressing the distinctive oral dynamics of Jesus' language.

> This language was not only the spoken word but personal address; it was not only in the indicative mode but in the imperative; it was not only in the third person but in the second and the first; it

> was not only a matter of declaration but of dialogue. (p. 12)

Similarly, another student of gospel rhetoric, Robert Tannehill (1975) stresses the forceful manner in which Jesus addressed people--not in polite and reasonable language but in extreme, direct, highly personal attack (pp. 115-116). These rhetorical descriptions give a sense of that quality of Jesus' speech which we characterize as immediacy.

The source of this immediacy lies in three conditions or factors (among others)--orality, eschatology, and personality. We must first of all remember the *oral* mode of Jesus' language--it was not written but spoken, and spoken *to* someone. Second, his language bespoke an eschatological sense and an eschatological message: Turn away from your sins, for the Kingdom of God is already coming! (cf. Mk. 1.15). That turn of phrase does not allude to a remote and lofty constellation but points down to something happening right now--imminence, crisis, event and urgency. Third, Jesus' personality informed his speaking. We do not know Jesus' personality. But we know that he was an intense, urgent person. The presence of this speaker, his sense of crisis, and his oral address all lay behind the immediacy of Jesus' way of speaking.

When we rotate these three factors and apply them to our present experience of Jesus' language, they disappear; and with them departs the immediacy of Jesus' way of speaking. Jesus' language as we now experience it no longer has oral address, no more eschatological acuteness, and not much left of the person who spoke it. First of all we are exceedingly remote from the speech situation--remote in tongue, time, place, and culture. But further, we are scarcely in a speech situation at all. We meet Jesus' way of speaking now not as oral speech but as a *read text*. Moreover, we read Jesus' language or we hear it read in a stylized circumstance--e.g., a sacred text, a portentous anticipation, a reverent approach, a delicate reading, a passive reception, and a familiar repetition. The action is liturgical. The language is devotional and declamatory. The eschatological crisis has passed. The person of the speaker is gone, elevated into a personage. It requires of us an unusual effort to experience the immediacy of Jesus' way of speaking.

Immediacy is the direct, personal, and urgent way that Jesus spoke to people on the spot. He spoke face-to-face with someone on the spot, addressing and pressing the person before him. These are the qualities with which Jesus once uttered what have now become his "teachings." But they are not the sayings of Confucius, the laws of Moses, the ways of Buddha, nor the saws of the Wise or the cries of the Prophet. They are not dictated, orated, promulgated, enunciated, ejaculated. They are spoken on the spot to someone, directly, personally, urgently--with an immediacy that is characteristic and distinctive of Jesus' way of speaking.

Congruence

To a remarkable extent the features of Jesus' language are consistent among themselves and with other aspects of his teaching. That is the quality of *congruence*, the fittingness of form and content, of language and teaching. Congruence is revealed in six selected features that we have already described in detail.

(1) *Sound*

Here we saw striking examples of sound befitting sentiment and image expressed, as well as purpose and audience addressed. Congruence of sound and these other aspects is revealed in Jesus' repetition of vowels and consonants, plays on words, rhythms and rhymes, where in each case the particulars of sound accord with the particulars of sentiment, image, purpose, and audience. Several of these features could be seen in one and the same saying, suggesting a congruence among sonal features themselves as well as congruence between sonal features and other aspects of expression. Double congruence is seen in the case of puns, where Jesus' striking juxtaposition of images was doubled by his striking juxtaposition of words (gnat/*galma* vs. camel/*gamla*). Here the *X* vs. *Y* of sense is expressed in precisely an *X* vs. *Y* of sound (rather than, say, *A* vs. *B*). These sonal features are *characteristic* of Jesus' way of speaking, not isolated instances. To that extent congruence is a characteristic quality of his language, at least in its sonal aspects.

(2) *Structure*

The characteristic structure of Jesus' language is parallelism of members, predominantly of the *antithetical* type, with a distinctive stress on the second member. The stress serves to emphasize not only that part of the saying which is *Jesus'* own teaching but also its *opposition* to the thesis in the first part. Hence we find congruence between structure and content. On a yet broader view we find congruence between structure and teaching style. Just as the structure of Jesus' sayings parallels by antithesis the traditional and common view, so also do the message and person of the teacher stand in antithesis to the traditional and contemporary. The x vs. y structure of his sayings, with stress on the y of Jesus' view, is congruent with the larger X vs. Y of his whole teaching style. That is, Jesus' teaching is Antithesis writ large. Hence the structure of his language, no less than its sound, is congruent with his teaching.

(3) *Form*

Jesus characteristically formulated his teaching in parables, figures of speech, and illustrations. These forms befit in a general way the kind of non-intellectual message that he taught. But at a specific level his illustrations depict things happening, people doing things, process and event and action, even drama. His parables too are images of action. Moreover, the parables invite re-action by failing to specify the punch-line or attitude to be taken towards the action depicted. This parabolic form nicely befits the content of the teaching. The "Kingdom of God" which Jesus taught is an action-event, just as the parable is action-image; like the parable, the "Kingdom" is something to be responded to in action. Put otherwise, the content of Jesus' teaching, like the parabolic form he gave to it, is not static but dynamic, not propositional but actional, not passive-reactive but active and participative. As such, the parabolic form also befits the purpose and audience of the teaching: not to transmit knowledge or convince of a point, but to excite responsive involvement; not for those with specialized talents, but for everyone. Hence we find for form, as we did for sound and structure, an impressive degree of congruence between Jesus' language and other aspects of his teaching.

(4) *Immediacy*

Immediacy refers to the dynamics of Jesus' way of speaking to someone. This quality of his language is congruent at least with the immediacy of his message and the response he sought. By contrast, it is possible for a speaker to treat such a message in non-immediate language: to speak formally, in stylized circumstances rather than on-the-spot; to speak obliquely rather than directly; to speak aloofly rather than urgently; to speak at and over an audience rather than to someone face-to-face; and so on. Indeed, that very kind of language is typical enough of sermons, lectures, and seminars about things that were once of surpassing moment: utterly remote language is used to teach a subject of utmost immediacy. In Jesus' case we find immediacy of language for immediacy of subject.

(5) *Originality*

Originality refers to the innovative features of Jesus' language. In brief, these linguistic features are congruent with the distinctive content of his teaching. For example, his language for God and the "Kingdom of God" was as original as what he said about them. Jesus' novel words and usages befitted the novel things he said and the new way that he urged people to do things. By contrast, it is possible for a speaker to talk about novel things in accustomed ways. Indeed, familiar language is expressly recommended to teachers for helping students learn unfamiliar concepts (e.g., Ausubel, 1963). With Jesus, however, we find original language for original message.

(6) *Variety*

Variety characterizes nearly the whole of Jesus' language. It befits the occasionalness of his teaching, the range of people he taught, and the openness of his message. For example, Jesus taught everywhere, not in designated places; all the time, not at specified hours; and to everyone, not to special people. Specialized or restricted language would not be conducive to this teaching, all the more so because of the content. The "Kingdom of God" denoted an event in which all people were to participate. Jesus was notorious for teaching that even pariahs like extortionists and thieves, and marginal people like women and children, all were included in the "Kingdom."

Moreover, no special talent was required in order to learn what Jesus taught. A "student" of Jesus did not *need* to know rabbinical Hebrew, nor *need* to have agricultural experience. Jesus taught in both rabbinical and pastoral language, to both refined and rustic audiences, in both structured and occasional circumstances. By contrast, quite specialized language, preparation, and disposition are required to learn from the teaching of Socrates and Confucius, for example, indeed from most teachers. The language of even the elementary classroom *must be learned* (e.g., Bellack et al., 1966), along with the many behaviors peculiar to being a student. With Jesus, however, one is not required to know a special language or to adopt a particular behavior. The variety of language permitted anyone to learn what he was teaching. Hence in its variety Jesus' language was congruent with his teaching, the content and audience, and with his teaching style.

* * * *

Variety, originality, and immediacy refer to features which are impressively congruent with other aspects of Jesus' teaching, just as the sound, structure, and form of his language are also congruent with the message, purpose, and audience of his teaching, and with his teaching style generally. Thus we come to the suggestive conclusion that congruence is a prominent overall quality of Jesus' pedagogical language.

Rhetorical Issues

Not all of the rhetorical qualities of Jesus' language are evident. Some remain at issue. Here we inquire into five selected issues under headings of simplicity, spontaneity, memorableness, remarkableness, and effectiveness.

In order to elicit the issues, we shall have recourse to some conclusions of the Aramaic scholar Matthew Black (1967). In exhibiting his conclusions as quoted below, Black implicitly addresses the five matters of interest here--the simplicity of Jesus' language, its degree of spontaneity, its memorableness, remarkableness, and effectiveness.

> Jesus did not commit anything to writing, but by His use of poetic form and language he ensured that his sayings would not be forgotten. The impression they make in Aramaic is of carefully premeditated and studied deliverances; we have to do with prophetic utterance of the style and grandeur of Isaiah, cast in a medium which can express in appropriate and modulated sound the underlying beauty of the sentiment or the passion out of which the thought arose--soft and gentle in the kindly sayings, as in the promise to the heavy-laden, inexorable and hard in the sayings about Offences, strongly guttural and mockingly sibilant where hypocrites and 'the rest of men' are contrasted with the Christian disciples. (p. 185)

Against this view we will set the conclusions of other scholars. Amos Wilder (1971) finds, for example, that Jesus' speech "is naive, it is not studied; it is *extempore* and directed to the occasion" (p. 12). Hence the issues arise. We begin with the simplicity of Jesus' language.

Simplicity

On the face of it, simplicity does not appear to characterize the kind of language whose features and qualities were just described. Yet simplicity is a descriptor most commonly applied to Jesus' language (e.g., Curtis, 1943; Griffith-Jones, 1914; Manson, 1935; Ross, 1904; Wilson, 1975). "Observe his Simplicity," noted Burrell (1902); "He advanced no abstruse propositions and used no sesquipedalian phrases" (p. 18). Black, however, finds style and grandeur in Jesus' sayings, studied deliverance, and modulated sound fitted to sentiment (1967, p. 185). Similarly, Wilder (1971) finds in Jesus' parables "art beyond art in the telling" (p. 77). In what sense can Jesus' language be said to be simple, and in what way not? To what extent does "simplicity" describe his speech, and to what aspects of it does that word apply?

Our review of Jesus' linguistic features may well have left the impression that this language is just not simple--not in its forms, their variety, richness, and match of sound, structure, sentiment, etc. Those writers who do call Jesus' language simple may be referring to characteristics other than these, such as concrete rather than abstract, everyday vs. arcane, pictorial vs. conceptual, illustrated vs. propositional, obvious vs. abstruse, and brief vs. expansive. In short, they say that it is easy to understand. The language is described as though couched and adapted so as to make a difficult subject matter easy to grasp (notionally) by an audience of a limited mental capacity. For example, Jesus used concrete language because he "knew that the disciples were not prepared to receive his teaching in abstract form"--they had "little or no education," were "too dull of comprehension," and showed "inability to do a bit of inductive reasoning" (McKoy, 1930, p. 63). Accordingly:

> His language was uniformly simple, clear, and concise. While the ideas conveyed were of the most profound nature, yet ... even the dullest minds could not fail to understand something of their meaning. (p. 98)

Similarly, the simplicity of Jesus' illustrations and stories allowed him to reach his audiences at their level of understanding, in which they were "as children"; so Jesus gave them 'milk' until they were ready for 'meat' (Wilson, 1975, p. 89). Such passages as these are typically held to show Jesus' use of the principle of adapting instruction to the capacity of the pupils.

Some of the characteristics cited for Jesus' language may well apply, but in the first place Jesus' message is not one of intellectual content, nor does it require an intellectual response. Moreover, Jesus spoke to cultured and educated people as well as to the ruder sort; many people, including his own family and closest associates, still did not understand or at least accept what he was saying; and Jesus generally refused to explain what he had said. Thus this particular usage of "simplicity" fails in large measure to describe Jesus' language. It does not entirely fail to describe, but rather fails to describe entirely, or adequately. For example, Jesus' language is stated to be easy vs. hard to understand, yet many people found it not easy to understand. The everydayness of Jesus' language is cited for its simplicity, whereas some of his language is clearly uncommon and unusual. Some further examples will illustrate this point.

(a) His everyday *illustrations* drawn from home and nature are often cited as evidence of simplicity (e.g., Griffith-Jones, 1914, p. 56). Yet Jesus' illustrations range far beyond the homey and agricultural, and many of them refer to things that are clearly not of the everyday sort (see Table 11).

(b) Jesus' *diction* is said to be simple, words drawn from the vocabulary of the people and not the scholar (Ibid.). Yet it was particularly Jesus' use of words that was uncommon, not only in the unusual usage of common words but also in the unusual combinations of common sounds and senses.

(c) Jesus' *vocabulary* is said to be simple and limited, not more ample than that of a child or peasant (Curtis, 1943, p. 105). Yet not only did Jesus wield this vocabulary in uncommonly mature and sophisticated ways, but also he spoke a good part of his language while conversing with people of a wide range of types and backgrounds, while disputing with experts in the technical rabbinical style, and while enunciating vituperation and invective. This is not the "gentle Jesus, meek and mild," and this is not the language of a child or peasant.

Jesus' language can be described as simple in these senses only if all of the non-simple aspects of his language are ignored.

At issue was not whether Jesus' language is simple-or-not. Clearly, it can be said to be both. Rather we conclude that simplicity is not an appropriate descriptor. It is best not to speak of Jesus' language in terms of simplicity, unless to say that it is at least not well described as simple.

Spontaneity

How spontaneous was the language of Jesus? Their perfection of form suggests that to some extent his parables and sayings may have been not only thought out beforehand but also given their particular shape with a deliberate end in view. To Matthew Black (1967), Jesus' sayings give the impression of "carefully premeditated and studied deliverances" (p. 185). But to Amos Wilder (1971), Jesus' speech "is naive, it is not studied; it is *extempore* and directed to the occasion" (p. 12). Similarly, Gunther Bornkamm (1960) finds that Jesus' words "always convey the original freshness of real spontaneity" (p. 105).

Wilder cautions that modern categories can mislead us into associating perfection of form with "cool and polished workmanship," and eloquent outbursts with "unpremeditated inspiration and even ecstasy," whereas, he asserts (with Ernst Kasemann), we should recognize that "felicity and sophistication of form is perfectly compatible with prophetic and, indeed, extempore uterance" (pp. 80-81). Wilder does not suggest how that may be so. Others too have stressed Jesus' spontaneous production of utterly perfect speech, such as the parables, leading these authors not to question the spontaneity but to declare their admiration of Jesus' unexplained facility in combining perfection with spontaneity. Regarding the parable of the Good Samaritan, for example, one writer (Smart, 1969, p. 65) draws attention to

> the astonishing fact that this parable, which as a literary creation has the perfection of a poem in which every word is in its only possible place, was uttered on the spur of the moment to meet a concrete situation. It was not fashioned in hours of meditation and polished over a long period of time, and yet its phrases are like the facets of a diamond.

The same is said of the parable of the Two Debtors (p. 36).

In apparent support of the "spontaneous" view is the occasional character of Jesus' teaching and the variety of situations and auditors which he faced. Jesus cannot have designed a series of sayings and parables to have at the ready, now to deliver in this kind of situation and to that type of auditor when just such an occasion might arise, and still other sayings and parables, equally finished, appropriate to other situations and audiences when other occasions would arise. Yet one also wonders how such rhetorical variety could have been improvised. One suggestion from education has it that many of Jesus' epigrams "sprang spontaneously from his soul, but such spontaneity is itself the best evidence of careful preparation" (McKoy, 1930, p. 170).

On the "studied" view, Jesus must have engaged in some preparation. Robert Stein (1978, pp. 31-32) makes this argument:

> One can conclude that Jesus must have spent time in organizing his teaching and preparing its form, for unless we conclude that this poetic parallelism simply popped into his mind on the spur of the moment, we must conclude that Jesus carefully prepared 'for his classes.'

Indeed, writers on teaching method have stressed that, for a teacher to deliver a parable, "much thoughtful preparation is a crucial pre-requisite" (Colman, 1967, p. 49). Moreover, some kind of preparation, even practice, on Jesus' part--say, in the unknown period prior to his public appearance or during those frequent times when he would go off alone--seems necessary to postulate, in light of the resemblances of Jesus' parallelisms to those of the Old Testament, his juxtaposition of sounds and meanings, his range of figures of speech, his variety of illustrations, and his skill at rabbinical dialectic. At the same time, Jesus was known to be uneducated, to speak a northern (country?) dialect, and to come from a humble, even somewhat backward background.

Both sides of this issue address the same accomplished rhetoric of Jesus' parables and sayings. The one side finds that it is carefully premeditated and studied, in the grand style; the other side finds that it is occasional, extempore, and naive. On the first view, Jesus' careful preparation appears a necessary conclusion against the odd alternative that accomplished rhetorical forms simply came to him on the spur of the moment; on the second view, artistic premeditation appears an unnecessary conclusion given the odd premise that rhetorical sophistication is perfectly compatible with impassioned, extempore utterance. Both views have to account for Jesus' unprepossessing background and for the impressive variety of situations in which he delivered his sayings. One wonders how so many utterances so finely shaped could have been either carefully prepared or extemporaneously delivered in so many and various a situation, all occasional in origin and character, by someone of such an unaccomplished background. Perhaps we have to do here with a speaker of unusual gifts, with extraordinary resourcefulness as well as with uncommon habitual style.

Memorableness

At issue here is not whether Jesus' language is memorable or forgettable, for it is demonstrably both: the great majority of those who heard it forgot it, and a small number remembered it. But did Jesus shape his language in such a form so as to be remembered?

The issue of memorableness turns on whether the rhetoric of Jesus' utterance was to serve for future retention or for present action. In noting Jesus' preference for speaking in antithetic parallelisms, Joachim Jeremias (1971) suggested that "one reason for this is certainly the urgency of this way of speaking, and the ease with which it can be remembered" (p. 20). Let us take this statement to suggest two reasons, possibly opposed: (1) "the urgency of this way of speaking" suggests that it served the purpose of *present action*; (2) "the ease of remembering" served for *future retention*. Again our two paradigmatic scholars differ on this issue, Black representing the second view and Wilder the first.

(1) *Future retention*

Black (1967) notes that, although Jesus committed none of his sayings to writing, by using poetic form and language "he ensured that his sayings would not be forgotten" (p. 185). Other scholars specify that the rhythmic and symmetrical form of the sayings was "intended to make them easier to memorize" (Trocme, 1973, p. 38). Indeed, Burney repeatedly stated it as "obvious" that Jesus designed his sayings in parallelism, rhythm, and rhyme with the intention of aiding the memory. Of the rhythmical form of the Lord's Prayer, for example, he asked:

> Was it accidental that our Lord so composed it, or did He intentionally employ art in composition as an aid to memory? Surely the latter conclusion is correct. (p. 113)

Others further specify that Jesus prepared his sayings in parallel, easy-to-remember form with the intent of future retention.

> It is clear from his use of various kinds of parallelism that he did place his teaching in a form that would be easy to memorize. It is evident that in so doing Jesus intended that his listeners would not only be challenged to decision by his words but also retain them in their memory. (Stein, 1978, p. 32)

That is, from the fact that Jesus used a language form that is easy to memorize, it is inferred that he used such a form with the intention that his sayings be (easily) memorized and retained in the future. The future retention view can apply both before and after Jesus' lifetime, to people down through the ages. Or it can apply only to the disciples of Jesus as they went about spreading his sayings during his lifetime--"for sending out of the disciples, and not the catechesis of the later church" (Trocme, 1973, p. 39).

> Their rhythmic and symmetrical form, intended to make them easier to memorize, no doubt has another aim beside that. It is also meant to make preaching and teaching easier for those who went on tour. ... [Their preservation] was made possible only because they were memorized by the disciples for the purposes of their preaching ministry. (p. 38)

This notion has appealed to education writers. "By wrapping up His teaching in such a pictorial, poetic and portable form Jesus ensured that it would be remembered by His pupils" (Rixon, 1977, p. 54; also, Griffith-Jones, 1914; Wilson, 1975). "Jesus knew full well that sayings of this kind would linger in the memory longer than any long-drawn-out discourse" (McKoy, 1930, p. 57). Thus Jesus' use of "poetic" and epigrammatic language was intended to make his sayings easy to memorize and hence easier to teach, with the aim of ensuring that they would be preserved in future memory.

It can be noted that some of these conclusions are not entailed of necessity, whether logical or pragmatic, by the premises.

(a) Although Jesus' sayings are indeed memorable, since people have remembered them, they are also forgettable, since people have also forgotten them. From the fact that Jesus' language is remembered we cannot conclude that he intended it to be remembered, any more than we can conclude, from the fact that Jesus' language is forgotten, that he intended it to be forgotten.

(b) Although the "poetic" form of Jesus' sayings makes them easy to memorize, it also makes them particularly striking at the moment of hearing them. Thus Jesus could as well have cast them in such a form with the intent of creating a present effect instead of ensuring future retention.

(c) Although his sayings are easy to memorize, their ease of memorization does not necessitate that they be memorized. All kinds of easy-to-memorize things said by various figures have not been remembered, and many hard-to-remember things have been memorized. Moreover, as events turned out, it appears that the reasons for which the disciples eventually recurred to Jesus' sayings had little to do with the easy-to-memorize form of the original.

It seems that Jesus' intent of future retention is made to follow in a reverse way from the fact that some of his sayings have been retained in the future.

(2) *Present action*

When Jeremias noted the urgency of Jesus' way of speaking in antithetic parallelisms, he can be taken to suggest its function at the moment of speaking. This view follows from what is known of Jesus' historical character, and it requires a judgment about his sense of eschatology. From the way that Jesus spoke and conducted himself, together with what it was that he taught, it is inferred that Jesus regarded the world as coming to an end. He therefore spoke an urgent message, using an urgent form of language, in order to provoke listeners to *present action*.

Scholars from divergent historical perspectives agree that Jesus acted in an immediate, last hour. Gunther Bornkamm: "Jesus counted without any question on the imminent ending of the world" (1960, pp. 203-204); "This 'here and now' carries all the weight in Jesus' message" (1974, p. 151). Howard Marshall: "It is hard to avoid the impression that Jesus spoke as if the end might come within the lifetime of his hearers" (1977, p. 277). Werner Kummel: "Jesus again and again proclaimed in the most varied fashion the urgent imminence of the end" (1961, p. 151); "Jesus expected the coming of the Kingdom of God within the generation of his hearers" (p. 86). Consequently the view follows that Jesus' way of speaking could not have been intended for future retention, but rather for some present purpose.

In his study of Jesus' rhetoric, Wilder (1971) cites Jesus' eschatological view and goes on to speak of

> the intense urging with which he spoke to the immediate crisis and the face-to-face hearer. The incomparable felicity and patterning of his sayings is indeed evident, but this formal perfection is not a matter of mnemonics; it is the countersign of the most effective communication of the moment. (p. 15)

Contrary to the view of future inculcation and retention, Wilder concludes that "Jesus' word was for the present, the last hour" (p. 14). His speech "is not calculated to serve some future hour. This utterance is dynamic, actual, immediate, reckless of posterity; not coded for catechists or repeaters" (p. 13). Contrary to the view that Jesus used poetic form so that his disciples would preserve his sayings, Hans Conzelmann (1973) concludes that Jesus did not train his followers for the future: "the present discipleship is the only one" (p. 35).

Other authors, it should be noted, do not share these views of imminence and present discipleship. Canon Deane (1922) ascribed "tranquillity and poise" to Jesus' teaching: "His are not words fevered by the imminence of the end" but rather "He seems consciously to address disciples of a far future" (pp. 69, 70). Accordingly, for Deane, repetition is one of the salient aspects of Jesus' teaching method. He pictures the disciples grouped about Jesus, repeating his words and memorizing them sentence by sentence, for Jesus "would take care that they who were to transmit His Gospel knew by heart its essential truths" (p. 67).

Beginning with the same premise that Black cited (viz., Jesus wrote none of his sayings down), Eduard Schweizer (1971) goes on to state--not that Jesus nonetheless ensured, by using poetic language, that his sayings would be remembered, but: "It is also clear that the accurate preservation and transmission of his words meant nothing to him" (p. 4). Schweizer cites the divergent versions in which even crucial utterances of Jesus were actually transmitted -- notwithstanding, we may add, the easy-to-memorize form of the original. Thus the one view has it that Jesus wrote nothing down because he took care to speak in such a way that it would be remembered; the other view has it that Jesus wrote nothing down because he took no care that it be remembered. Still other authors have concluded that Jesus purposely wrote nothing down because he committed his teaching to the disciples, trusting in their faithful and scrupulous care to hand down his teachings (Ross, 1904, p. 27); or yet because he had no intention of giving his instructions a stereotyped form (Stevens, 1901, p. 19).

In sum, it may be that the rhetorical form of Jesus' sayings, though memorable, cannot be imputed to him as though an intentional usage for the purpose of future retention. Jesus spoke and acted in the present hour, which for him was the last hour; he therefore spoke urgently and immediately to people in the moment to provoke some present action. For Jesus, things were at an end--thus the striking form of his language. The contrary view maintains: For us, things are still going on--thus the striking form of Jesus' language; since we remember it, he intended that we remember it; and since we can remember it because it is so striking, he made it so striking in order that we could remember it.

The quality of Jesus' rhetoric has served to carry his sayings into the future, but that was not the aim which his rhetoric served, for he uttered his sayings for the present. Jesus' language is indeed memorable, but he does not seem to have intended it to be remembered.

Remarkableness

All scholars agree, and we ourselves can see, that Jesus' language is remarkable. Black (1967) speaks of its "style and grandeur," its impressive alliteration, assonance and paranomasia fitted to the image expressed (p. 185). Wilder (1971) speaks of the "rhetorical perfection" of Jesus' language, the "incomparable felicity" of his sayings, and the "art beyond art" of his parables (pp. 15, 77, 80). Burney (1925) and Jeremias (1971) describe the parallel structure of Jesus' sayings, the variety of devices used to achieve parallelism, and the different rhythmic stresses of his sayings for different purposes. Various scholars detail long lists of his different figures of speech (e.g., Horne, 1920; Stein, 1978) and range of illustrations (e.g., Griffith-Jones, 1914; Rixon, 1977). The evangelists themselves depict in a dramatic way Jesus' skillful disputation and his forceful vituperation. Thus there is no question that Jesus' language is remarkable in and of itself.

How remarkable is Jesus' language, not by itself but by comparison? Black (1967) likens his prophetic utterance to the grandeur of Isaiah (p. 185). Trocme (1973) speaks of his "remarkable gift of expression which makes Jesus the equal of the most brilliant wisdom writers" (p. 40). Others are led to conclude that Jesus "was, even beyond Socrates, to whom the palm is usually awarded, a master of dialectical skill" (Montague, 1884, p. 552), and a better questioner than Socrates (Horne, 1920, p. 205; Squires, 1927, p. 99). One wonders how it was that Jesus possessed such language, remarkable both in itself and by comparison.

The linguistic and cultural features of Jesus' setting reveal little that might account for the remarkable character of his language. On the contrary, they only reveal its remarkableness all the more. For, on the whole, Jesus' speech is original and distinctive. It stands out against the language and culture of his time, and it has few parallels either in the ancient traditions or in modern developments.

Of course, Jesus did not invent the tongue which he spoke. He spoke a recognizably Palestinian language expressing a recognizably Jewish culture. At issue is the manner in which he spoke. Jesus broke into the world of speech of his time, says Wilder (1971), "with a novel and powerful utterance.

... There was here a new dynamics in human speech" (p. 9). Jesus' manner of speaking was so different that Trocme (1973) terms it "Jesus' radical freedom of speech" (p. 78). A great part of this distinctiveness attaches to what it was that Jesus said and to the manner of the person who was saying it. But here we emphasize, to the extent that inevitably artificial distinctions will permit, the character of the language forms expressing Jesus' message and person. The language itself, no less than the character of teacher and subject, is remarkable.

Heard within the contemporary setting, Jesus spoke in unexpected ways. As we saw earlier, his originality is revealed in six characteristics which find no contemporary analogy (Jeremias, 1971, pp. 29-37).

(1) The parallel *sayings* of Jesus, by contrast to traditional and contemporary usage, apply to a wide range of contexts and lay unusual stress on the second part of the saying rather than on the first.

(2) Unlike teachers of the time, Jesus spoke *riddles*.

(3) The *parables* of Jesus are unique to him, in their non-fabular, non-allegorical character, and in their simplicity, clarity, and brevity--"all this is without analogy" (p. 30)

(4) The phrases which Jesus used to express his central theme of the coming Kingdom of God (e.g., *malkuta*) have no parallels in the language of Jesus' contemporaries or in the entire Jewish tradition. That indicates Jesus' "power to create new eshatological language" (p. 34).

(5) Jesus' use of the prefacing *'amen* in his sayings is unique to him in the Jewish (as well as Christian) tradition, and this usage was recognized at the time to be unusual and distinctive of Jesus. "Here we have the creation of a new expression by Jesus" (p. 36).

(6) Jesus' use of the caritative form of the word for father, *'abba*, to address God "is the most important linguistic innovation on the part of Jesus" (p. 36).

All of these points reveal the remarkableness of Jesus' language. It is remarkable in itself and by comparison, in the contemporary linguistic and cultural context. Some accounting for this remarkableness seems called for. What is the origin of this language? How did Jesus come by it?

When we compare Jesus' language to his personal background we find it still more remarkable. The greater part of Jesus' life is unknown, including his personal development. But it is known that people at the time, citing his unremarkable origin, wondered over the way he taught (Mk. 6.2-3). He was known to come from a large family and an insignificant place; he was known to be a (or son of a) carpenter; he was known to be uneducated; and he was heard to speak a dialect of the rural north. Nothing is known of his appearance, but it likely was not the appearance typical of a religious or social personage--teacher, priest, lawyer, leader. He was known to have belonged for a time to the group around John the Baptist but he was also known not to practice the asceticism and worldly-withdrawal into wilderness of the Baptist's group; to the contrary, Jesus was well-known for associating with all social types, and he was publicly accused of being a glutton, drunkard, and friend of prostitutes and thieves (Mt. 11.19). Hence we learn nothing from his origins, family, dialect, education, appearance, or social habits which might help account for his remarkable language.

On the other hand, we can turn the issue around and ask: Were his background different from what it was, would that then explain his remarkable language? Suppose Jesus had been born of a cultured, socially prominent family in the south, say in Jerusalem; suppose that he had been given a university education, theological training as a rabbi or lawyer; suppose that he had grown up to speak a learned dialect, to dress and groom after the best fashion, and to associate only with the better class of people;--yet, we might think, all of that could as easily have impoverished his language, muting it to indistinctness; and even with all of that, still we might wonder over the sources of his extraordinary linguistic turn, a turn which brought him well beyond mastery of language to an unparalleled manipulation of its forms and to inventiveness of form and usage. Perhaps there is no accounting for it. Of any other figure we could say without prejudice that he was an inspired speaker.

Effectiveness

What effect did Jesus' language have on those who heard it? This last and ultimately crucial issue proves difficult not only to resolve but also to define. Of concern here is the distinction between our response to Jesus' language and the reaction of those who heard him at the time. What was their response, not ours?

We know in a general but clear way that people who heard Jesus were struck by his manner of speaking. We know too that many people were offended by his way of speaking (e.g., *'abba*). A relatively small number of people are known to have been shocked but attracted. Thus, if we consider the effectiveness of Jesus as a teacher, we can think it minimal (see Dillon, 1981a). If on the other hand we consider the accomplishment of his language, we must think very highly of it indeed. But what of its effect?

When scholars speak in terms of the effect of Jesus' language, they use without exception words denoting positively strong, clear, and direct impact. For example:

- "By a variety of means the Gospels speak with strong personal impact" (Tannehill, 1975, p. 27).
- The strophic form of Jesus' sayings "produces an effect of singular intensity and dramatic power" (Manson, 1935, p. 55).
- His paradoxical sayings "strike the ear and arrest special attention" (Stevens, 1901, p. 38).
- His parables "arrest the hearer" and "compel response" (Dodd, Funk, in Perrin, 1976, pp. 133, 139).
- His speech had the character "of compelling imagination, of spell, of mythical shock and transformation" (Wilder, 1971, p. 84).

But what must be noted about all of these descriptions is the likelihood that, although they propose to describe the effect of Jesus' language, they cannot properly be taken to describe its effect on Jesus' auditors but rather must be taken to refer to the effect which Jesus' language has on those who are writing the descriptions. Norman Perrin (1976) illustrates this point. He says of the parables that "they constantly shatter and probe, disturb and challenge," and then he continues with: "in ways which are for me personally analogous to the impact of great art" (p. 200). Strong and undeniable though these present effects be on these modern (and Christian) authors, we must yet inquire whether they are also the effects which Jesus' language had on people at the time.

In general, our inquiry into this issue is frustrated by the nature of the evidence available for addressing it. Little can be known in a specific way of the effects which Jesus' language had on his contemporaries, for little specific reaction of any kind is depicted in the gospel texts for the greater part of what Jesus said (Dillon, 1981a). That is, we must imagine the effect. Thus, for example, these imagined effects: "When the Master lectured the people listened and learned, were informed and stirred, and their lives were enriched" (Price, 1946, p. 110). Rather than speculate on this matter, we can review the evidence we do have.

First, we know in a general but clear way that, at least initially, the effect of Jesus' way of teaching was "amazement" or wonderment. "The people who heard him were amazed at the way he taught, for he wasn't like the teachers of the Law; instead, he taught with authority" (Mk. 1.22). Part of Jesus' "authority" and contrast with other teachers surely derived from the distinctiveness of his language (e.g., *'amen*, parables). We can say that Jesus' language was striking, i.e., had a striking effect on those who heard it.

Further, we know that Jesus' parables and riddles, his terminology for the "Kingdom of God," and his stress on the second member of his parallel sayings, all were peculiar at the time and probably striking and/or intriguing to some people. More specifically we can say that Jesus' use of *'abba* for God was striking to his contemporaries. Some of them were drawn to it and adopted it for themselves; most were offended by it and deliberately avoided using it. His use of *'amen* to preface his sayings was also striking. All who heard it recognized it as assertive; some found it authoritative and most found it presumptuous; no one adopted it. In these cases we find that Jesus' language had a striking but also shocking effect, mostly in the negative sense of 'shocking.'

Third, his dialectical language is seen to have a clear enough effect. Few of his arguments are shown to be convincing, but those made in retort to critics are seen to arouse enmity and shame (see the *a fortiori* in Lk. 13.15-17). Similarly, his invective was shown to be insulting (e.g., Lk. 11.45). And the effect of his counter-questions is made particularly clear: they frustrated his questioners, shamed and silenced them, deepening their already negative reaction to the speaker (for details see Dillon, 1981b).

As for the rhetorical qualities we have noted, the variety of Jesus' language probably had little effect. The variety is remarkable *to us* rather than to those who heard Jesus. To the majority of Jesus' auditors the variety of his language (e.g., figures of speech, illustrations, modes of discourse) could not have been evident and hence could not have had much effect. Only those in a position to hear or to review a good sample of Jesus' speech would even have noticed its variety. That is not the case, however, with the immediacy of his way of speaking, which must have been evident to anyone who spoke with Jesus. Indeed, it must have been unavoidable. The effect of his personal, direct, and urgent address seems to have been to require a response, perhaps to provoke one. With significant individual exceptions, the response was predominantly negative or non-positive (including the case of the wealthy man, Mk. 10.21-22). It is fair to say that the urgency of Jesus' way of speaking did not have a correspondingly urgent effect on most people who heard him.

Finally, those features of sound and form which we have qualified as congruence must have made some kind of impression, after the manner of a succinct, well-turned expression. The clearest evidence we have is the fact that a good sample of Jesus' speech was remembered by those who heard it. But here we run into the problem of circularity around which the issue of "memorableness" turned. On that point we must appreciate that during Jesus' lifetime a "memorable effect" may not have been intended and could not logically have come into force; and we must bear in mind the complementary fact that, while some remembered, most people who heard Jesus forgot what he said. Thus one of the most evident features of Jesus' language--its form, of ease to memorize--turns out to have little enough effect: not at the time and not on the majority of auditors.

In sum, the evidence we have for the effect of Jesus' language is scanty and mixed, inevitably entangled with the reaction given to message and speaker. The language can be seen to be striking at the time, but mostly in a negative way, and it later proved memorable for some, but forgettable for most. The positive case which most scholars seek to build rests on the effect not for auditors of the time but for themselves who are describing the effect or who are imagining it. Moreover, the effect they describe presupposes a favorable disposition towards Jesus (e.g., Christian faith). One wonders if Jesus' language has an effect only on those already affected by him. For the vast remainder, whether in the 1st or the 20th century, when Jesus' way of speaking is not found offensively shocking or merely striking, it can be judged as highly accomplished language oddly lacking in effect.

Summary and Conclusion

At the start of this long venture we set out to describe and then to evaluate the language of Jesus as a teacher, with an interest in its pedagogical rather than theological features.

Descriptive findings

(1) As for the *tongue* which Jesus spoke, he may have known something of Hebrew and Greek but he characteristically taught in his native Aramaic.

(2) The *sound* of Jesus' (Aramaic) language was characterized by repetition of vowels and consonants, by word-plays, and by certain patterns of rhythm and to an extent rhyme; and further these features of sound varied in accordance with the sense expressed and/or with the purpose and audience being addressed. That is, different teachings were modulated in appropriately different sounds.

(3) The characteristic *structure* of Jesus' language was parallelism of members, predominantly of antithetical type, where the second, distinctly

Jesuan part of the saying stands in opposition to the first part. In general, Jesus structured his sayings as: "You have heard it said that *X* is the case, but now I tell you that anti-*X* is the case." Antithetical parallelism also characterizes Jesus' style of teaching: he and his message, no less than this language, stand in antithesis to the traditional and contemporary.

(4) As to the *form* of Jesus' language we found no one characteristic form. He gave form to his teaching in any number of types of figures of speech; in shorter, example-like parables and longer, story-like ones; in a great range of illustrations depicting all manner of events and people; in various types of argument and vituperation--but in disputation the particular form of counter-question; and in all modes of discourse, including the more extended narrative and discursive modes as well as the interactive modes of conversation, discussion, and question-answer exchanges.

Evaluative findings

To characterize Jesus' language, we selected four qualities: its variety, originality, immediacy, and congruence.

(1) *Variety*. Other terms are more colorful but less encompassing and even less characteristic, especially "poetry." The variety of Jesus' language suggests the mastery with which he commanded and manipulated sound, structure, and form.

(2) *Originality*. Jesus invented as well as manipulated. Heard against the linguistic setting of his day, his language was original in some features of his parallel sayings and riddles; in most features of his parables; and in all features of speaking about his central theme of the "Kingdom of God," in his language for God (*'abba*), and in his use of *'amen* to preface his sayings.

(3) *Immediacy*. It was characteristic of Jesus that he spoke on-the-spot to people, directly and personally face-to-face, urgently pressing upon them his message.

(4) *Congruence* describes the fittingness of form and content, language and teaching. An impressive degree of congruence appears both within the

linguistic features of sound, structure, and form, and more generally between linguistic features and other aspects of Jesus' teaching style, such as his message, purpose, and audience. To some extent as well the qualities of variety, originality, and immediacy of language befit corresponding qualities of Jesus' message, purpose, and audience.

Unresolved issues

We then identified five further qualities of Jesus' language as issues remaining unresolved.

(1) The *simplicity* of Jesus' language seems undecidable. It is probably not a useful descriptor to apply.

(2) The *spontaneity* of Jesus' language remains undecided. There are good arguments to be made from the linguistic evidence that his language was both studied and naive, premeditated and extempore.

(3) The *memorableness* of Jesus' language is a foreclosed issue in that it was remembered, but the issue again arises in that the language was also forgotten by most people who heard it. At issue is whether Jesus so phrased his teaching as to intend that it be retained in future memory, or rather that it provoke present action. Here the linguistic evidence is used to support both sides of the issue, so theological and pedagogical presuppositions are invoked to resolve it either way--though not always in a logical way.

(4) The *remarkableness* of Jesus' language remains to be accounted for. How did he come by mastery and originality of language? Nothing we know about him explains that. In such a case it is permissible and customary to say that the speaker is inspired; yet saying just that about Jesus fruitlessly evokes theological/devotional prejudices pro and con, thereby failing to advance the issue.

(5) The *effectiveness* of Jesus' language is difficult to determine. There is no question that his language was highly accomplished. But there is no evidence that his language was highly effective. Its effect on auditors remains largely unknown, while the greater part of what is known suggests a negative

effect. Perhaps the most that can be said is that his language was often striking. What is most said in the literature, however, is the detailed, positive impact of Jesus' language; the authors may be describing its effect on themselves rather than on those who heard Jesus speak.

Conclusion

Jesus' language was even more highly accomplished than much of the literature depicts it to be. For example, the literature's emphasis on parables neglects the variety and richness of forms which his language took; the emphasis on simplicity neglects its impressively complex juxtapositions of sound, structure, form, and content; the emphasis on homey illustrations neglects the range of sophisticated references; the emphasis on rustic vocabulary neglects the rabbinical diction; the emphasis on lyric and pastorale neglects the range of argument, dialectic, and invective; the emphasis on poetry neglects the force and urgency of his personal address and the varied modes of his expression. To a greater extent than is commonly remarked, Jesus' language was varied, original, immediate and forceful; the whole language congruent with the content, purpose, and audience of his teaching.

Therefore Jesus' language is accomplished not just rhetorically but furthermore pedagogically. It is on this point that Jesus has been both underrated and overestimated. On the whole, New Testament studies take adequate notice of his language but miss the pedagogy of it; education sources take inadequate note of the language and exaggerate the pedagogy. In our view Jesus *taught* in far finer *language* than heretofore represented; the language was not only accomplished in itself but impressively conducive to the teaching.

Nonetheless the language had *uncertain educational effect*. It is incorrect to stare at the language and, while admiring its ipsative quality, to state that it had a corresponding transitive effect. We should hesitate to attribute to those who heard Jesus teach a quality of response which corresponds to the quality we ascribe to his language, not to say his message and person. Jesus spoke wonderfully when he taught. That is one thing. How people were influenced by his way of speaking, and what they learned as a result of it--that is another thing. Many people were unmoved when not repulsed by Jesus' wonderful way of speaking.

We conclude that Jesus' pedagogical language was highly accomplished, perhaps surpassing that of most other teachers. More so than the literature allows, Jesus spoke his teaching in pedagogically complete language; but less so than it claims did Jesus' language accomplish an educationally complete result. Who, in fact, learned from it? - and what did they learn? (chapter 7)

Chapter 7

RESULT IN LEARNING

As far as can be seen, few of the people whom Jesus taught learned what he was teaching them. Many more people, including some whom he had taught, subsequently came to learn a great deal. But their learning cannot be seen as a result of Jesus' teaching activity, nor as something that Jesus taught.

Who learned what Jesus taught them? The question of learning turns out to be quite unexpectedly complicated. It is easy enough to answer, but wrongly. The first thing to do is to set forth the terms of the question that is being asked.

The Question of Learning

In its general formulation, the question of learning runs: *Who learned what from the teaching*? That is a simple question but oddly difficult to answer, correctly. For, a rider to this question runs, *And how can we tell*?--or, how do we know who learned, what they learned, and that what they learned is a result of the teaching (and not of something else)?

That is a tough question to answer reliably in the everyday practice of education, as in determining what schoolchildren have learned. Educational researchers and practitioners struggle to construe an answer out of a mass of evidence gathered from an array of techniques applied to the evaluation of the learning of the children before them. In the case before us here, few of the learners can even be identified for evaluation, most of the techniques cannot be applied, and little evidence can be gathered out of which an answer can be construed. The eventual answer will turn on saying either that there was little learning (who learned what?) or that there is little evidence of learning (how can we tell?). One answer that does *not* turn out is, there was a lot of learning.

Main Question

Who learned what from Jesus' teaching? (and, how do we know that?)

"*From Jesus' teaching*" signals that the learning in question is a result of the teaching, and the teaching of Jesus, and not of something or somebody else. Students commonly learn things that are not learned as a result of the teaching; often enough they may even learn opposite or unrelated things as well as some things intended by the teacher. Thus to answer the question it is not enough to assess what students have learned; a line must somehow be established that traces what they learned back to the teaching, and to other factors of which the learning is a result. Who learned as a result of Jesus' teaching?

"*Who*" signals the identity and number of those learning this or that thing. How many of the people whom Jesus taught learned what he taught them? Which types or grouping of people learned what?--e.g., disciples, Pharisees.

"*What*" signals the thing that is learned. Always it is a matter of learning something which was not taught as well as learning the thing taught. In Jesus' case, the substance of the teaching was the subject matter, "Kingdom of God," and the aim, "Repent!" Who learned the Kingdom of God? Who repented? (Mk 1.15) or, Who did what God wanted him to do? (Mk 3.35) In the second place, What else was learned? That would include things opposite to the Kingdom of God or Repent, or things related and unrelated to that teaching. What is it that was learned?

Subsidiary Questions

As just made clear, the question of learning does not stand by itself but in relation to other common questions of education--most broadly the question of teaching but more pointedly questions about the learner (who?) and the subject matter (what?), for example. The question of learning *cannot arise* of itself, and cannot be answered without implicating at the same time a series of other questions in other commonplace categories to which the category of learning is related. There is no choice in this matter but to identify at least the generic questions in these other categories insofar as they arise by entailment of the question of learning. These questions will be seen as themselves interrelated as well as related to learning.

1. *Substance of teaching.* (a) To what extent or degree was the *subject-matter* that Jesus taught learned? (the Kingdom of God). Put otherwise: Of that which was learned, what part was the subject matter that Jesus taught? (b) To what extent did the learning correspond to his *aim* in teaching (Repent). Otherwise put: What part of that which was learned did Jesus not aim at?--whether opposite or unrelated to his aim.

2. *Circumstance of teaching.* What was learned in which milieu? How did the milieux, greater or lesser, impinge upon the learning?

3. *Activity of teaching.* What was learned as a result of Jesus' various *actions* of teaching, and the various *language forms* of teaching? At a crass level this question reduces to: How effective was this or that teaching technique?

4. *Correspondents of teaching.* This category of "learner" subsumes many questions when related one-by-one to the other common categories.

(a) Jesus had an aim in teaching, but so did his correspondents; what were *the learners' aims*, and how did their aims affect the learning that resulted?

(b) Other telling questions concern *characteristics* of the learners: What was their status or grouping, and how might that have impinged on their learning? What dispositions--attitudes, beliefs, "personality"--regarding the teacher and the subject matter did the learners bring to the teaching?

(c) What was *the learners' activity* in the teaching-learning situation, as they inter-acted with the teacher over subject matter in circumstance?

(d) One key specific question asks about the *learners' responses* or reactions to the teaching, for from that some evidence of learning can be deduced. How did the learners respond?

5. *The teacher.* What part did Jesus play in the learning that resulted? Which of the learning can be attributed to him? As has been seen--in the previous paragraph if nowhere else--the question of learning is not co-terminous with the question of teaching; the result in learning is neither the final nor the whole word on the quality of the teaching. What is being evaluated here is *the learner* and the *learning.* The question of teaching will be reserved for the asking in the next chapter (e.g., How good a teacher was Jesus?).

The questions just listed are formulated examples of the kinds of question implicated by the main question of learning. A major problem in answering the main question is that the answer will of necessity *also* answer the subsidiary questions. What commonly happens is that these subsidiary questions are not explicitly asked; they are answered anyway.

Thus, both in today's education and in the case of Jesus, we can hear resounding answers to the major question of learning, which confound that question with the question of teaching and tangle it all around with unwitting answers to unasked related questions.

A major problem still remains, to find a way to answer the question. *How can we tell* who learned what from the teaching? In Jesus' case this methodological problem is altogether more difficult than in the case of schoolteachers today. We will look first at the New Testament texts to examine the evidence available and to construe it as showing that few people learned as a result of what Jesus was teaching them.

Evidence of Learning

In address to the question of learning, we turn first to the gospel texts for evidence of learning in response to Jesus' teaching activity. The search begins with specific responses and pursues successively broader ones, ending with the evidence in lifelong learning by contrast to the initial immediate responses to instances of Jesus' teaching.

Specific learning

In the synoptic texts bearing on the period between Jesus' first appearance as a teacher and his last gathering with disciples before his death, there are approximately 112 isolable units depicting a teaching episode--e.g., a dialogue encounter, a telling of parables. Each of these episodes depicts a teaching act by Jesus and a reaction from the people whom he was teaching. The reactions from these learners can be judged as either positive or negative or none (no reaction depicted). The results of this procedure are reported in Table 13 for the various types of respondents--crowds, groups, individuals, religious leaders, disciples. (For a detailed report of this study see Dillon, 1981a.)

Table 13 shows that a systematic inspection of the gospel texts reveals relatively few positive reactions to Jesus' teaching activity, and comparatively feeble ones at that. Moreover, no reaction at all is depicted in half of the cases, including half in each of the respondent categories. Of the remaining reactions, about half are positive, half negative. Thus not much evidence is available, and little enough evidence of positive reactions.

As to the quality of reactions, few enough of the positive ones give evidence of learning in direct relation to Jesus' teaching, and few show a marked degree of intensity. In the terms as depicted in Table 13, the reactions may be arranged on a scale from the merest to the most.

1. approach, welcome
2. listening, hearing
3. amazement, wonderment
4. understanding
5. commendation, acclamation
6. joy, praise/thanks to God
7. spreading the news
8. expectation of the Kingdom of God
9. promise of good deeds

10. offer to follow Jesus
11. following Jesus at call
12. following instructions
13. faith/worship of Jesus.

This display shows few reactions of an intense order, and fewer still in direct relation to what Jesus taught. Where are the reactions depicting people learning as taught?--e.g. repenting in face of the coming Kingdom?

The negative reactions, on the other hand, show these respondents clearly *not* learning what Jesus taught, and exhibiting intensity enough. Again in terms depicted (Table 13), the scale runs as follows.

1. refusal to receive Jesus
2. not understanding
3. fear
4. keeping quiet
5. grumbling
6. walking off
7. refusal to repent
8. refusal to follow
9. criticism, mockery, abuse
10. anger, rage
11. rejection of teaching
12. expulsion of the teacher
13. threats, traps
14. plots to arrest/kill Jesus.

The order of negative reactions appears both more intense and direct in responding to the teaching and in giving clear evidence of not-learning.

A complementary inspection of the gospel texts rearranges the depicted reactions to reveal evidence of learning in response to various teaching techniques. These include the parables, polemical and pedagogical dialogues, and several subtypes each of questions, sayings, figures of speech, and miracles (as classified principally by Stein, 1978). The result is displayed in Table 14.

Table 13. Depicted Reactions, by Respondent Type*

Respondent	Positive Reactions (N=44)	Negative Reactions (N=29)	No Reaction (N=85)
1. Crowds	come to Jesus - Mk 3.8 acclamation - Mk 11.9 amazement at teaching -Mt 7.28-29, 22.33 amazement at healing -Mk 1.27, 2.12, 26, 5.42, 7.37; Lk 9.43; Mt 9.33, 15.31 rejoice - Lk 13.17 praise God - Lk 7.16, 18.43 expect Kingdom - Lk 19.11 wonderment - Lk 7.49	he's mad! - Mk 3.21 expel Jesus - Mk 5.17 not repent - Mt 11.20 grumbling - Lk 19.7	Mk 1.29, 40, 4.2, 5.25, 6.34, 7.25, 8.1, 22, 11.15, 12.37b Lk 12.16, 13.1, 6, 10, 22, 19.45 Mt 8.5, 9.27, 11.7, 13.24
2. Groups	amazement at teaching - Mk 1.22 amazement at healing - Lk 8.56	reject, lack faith - Mk 6. 3,6 not receive Jesus - Lk 9.53 anger, criticism - Mk 14.3 anger, threats - Lk 4.28-29	Lk 14.7, 7.11 (other 9) Mt. 11.2
3. Individuals	spread news of healing -Mk 1.45, Lk 8.39, Mt. 9.31 praise God over healing -Mk 2.25, Lk 13.13, 17.15, 18.43 listen to teaching - Lk 10.39 follow Jesus on road - Mk 10.52 welcome Jesus, promise good deeds - Lk 19.6-8	gloom, refusal to follow Jesus - Mk 10.22	Mk 1.23, 29, 2.6, 3.11, 5.21, 25, 7.25, 32, 8.22, 9.17, 14.3 Lk 7.11, 37, 10.38 (Martha), 12.13, 14.1 Mt 8.5, 9.32

Respondent	Positive Reactions (N=44)	Negative Reactions (N=29)	No Reaction (N=85)
4. Religious Leaders	amazement - Mk 12. 17 praise of answer - Mk 12.34, Lk 20.39 offer to follow Jesus - Mt. 8.18	plan to arrest/kill Jesus -Mk 3.6, 11.8, 12.12 criticize, lay traps - Lk 11.53-54 mock Jesus - Lk 16.14 accuse of demonology - Mt. 9.34 rage - Lk 6.11 shame - Lk 13.17 went away - Mt 22.22 kept quiet, unable to answer -Lk 14.6, 20.26	Mk 2.6, 15, 18, 23, 3.22, 7.1, 8.11, 10.2, 11.27, 14.3 Lk 7.36, 10.25, 14.7, 15.4, 8, 11, 16.19, 18.9
5. Disciples	follow Jesus at call -Mk 5.11, Lk 5.28, Mt 19.27 preach/heal as instructed -Mk 6.12-13, Lk 10.17 acclaim as messiah - Mk 8.29 hear Jesus - Mk 11.14 understand parables - Mt. 13.51-52 amazement - Mk 6.51 worship - Mt 14.33 offer to share in suffering - Mk 10.39	fear - Mk 4.41, 9.2, 32 anger, criticism - Mt. 26.8 rebuke by Peter - Mk 8.32 not understanding - Mk 6.52, 9.32 sadness - Mt 17.23	Mk 4.10, 26, 7.17, 8.14, 9.33, 38, 10.10, 13, 32, 11.20, 12.41, 13.1, 3, 14ff. Lk 16.1, 17.1ff, 18.1 Mt 8.21, 10.26ff, 17.24, 18.10, 21, 20.1, 24.45, 25.1, 14

*Source: Dillon 1981a

Here again the nature of the sources is that no reaction is depicted in the majority of cases, whether overall or for any category of technique. No reaction is depicted for half of the cases of miracles and questions, for 70% of the dialogue encounters, 80% of the figures of speech, 90% of the parables, and 100% of the parallel sayings. A separate study bearing on Jesus' questions (Dillon, 1981b), reveals that of all the *non*-rhetorical questions put by Jesus to people, two-thirds receive no response of any observable kind.

Thus there is little textual evidence of people learning in response to Jesus' teaching techniques. In each case the reactions are a mix of positive and negative, few enough of them positive.

The method pursued to this point is objectionable on several good grounds (for an extensive discussion see Dillon, 1981a). It is pursued here to see what evidence of learning can be found in the texts. The texts do not yield much evidence, and little positive evidence. In that way the procedure serves to raise the question of what evidence is available and where it may be found. Judgments in plenty have been made about the learning that resulted from Jesus' teaching activity; what is the procedure used in making such a judgment, on what grounds is it made, and what evidence is adduced in making it?

In search of other evidence of learning, further methods may be applied to the New Testament texts. Instead of examining the specifics of learning, these examine the broad response to Jesus, the selective response of his disciples, and the subsequent response to his teaching. They look respectively at the larger, the more focussed, and the developed picture of learning that may be drawn by the sources. The larger picture would show the *over-all learning* given in broad response to Jesus, rather than the specific reactions in this and that circumstance. The focussed picture would bear on the *select learning* of the disciples, rather than that of the diffuse and various collection of people whom he taught. The developed picture would reveal the *lifelong* learning as it later unfolded, rather than the immediate learning at the time of teaching.

Table 14. Depicted Reactions, by Teaching Technique*

Technique	Total Cases (N=186)	Positive (N=31)	Negative (N=19)	No Reaction (N=136)
1. Parables	ca. 50	Mt 13.51 (3 parables)	Mk 12.12 Lk 16.14	n=ca.45
2. Parallel sayings (3 types)	14**	-	-	n=14
3. Figures of speech (10 types)	29**	Mk 1.17 10.25	Mk 8.15 Lk 4.28 13.15	n=24
4. Dialogues	22	Mk 10.38-39 12.32-34 Lk 20.39	Mk 3.6 Lk 20.26 (+Mt 22.22) Mt 10.22	n=16
5. Questions	20**	Mk 8.19, 29 Lk 7.39 10.36 22.35 Mt. 17.25 21.31	Mk 3.4 11.33 Lk 14.3 Mt 12.11 12.27	n=8
6. Miracles (3 types)	51	Mk 1.23, 40 2.1 5.18-20 6.51 9.17 10.46, 52 14.33 Lk 7.16 8.56 13.10 17.11 Mt 9.27, 32 15.29	Mk 3.1 4.41 5.15-17 6.52 9.6 Lk 14.1	n=29

*source: Dillon 1981a
**a systematic sample of all cases

Overall learning

The larger picture broadly painted by the gospels themselves depicts an overall failure to learn what Jesus was teaching. The broad response was either lack of acceptance or positive rejection.

The case as clearly depicted is that the people whom Jesus taught gave the broad response of rejecting his message, his way of living his life, and his person (paraphrase of Schillebeeckx, 1979). The successively broader responses were rejection by his family, by synagogue congregations, by towns, by regions, by province, by religious groupings of all kinds, and by Judaism and "Israel" as a whole. (For details see chapter 4 on correspondents of teaching.)

Whereas entire named towns are depicted not to repent, no towns are depicted to repent. Among other positive broad responses not depicted are decisions and actions by groups of people in favor of the Kingdom of God; communities forming and living in expectation of the Kingdom as Jesus taught it; exemplary individuals acting in this and that way in response to having been taught by Jesus; outstanding reversals of attitude and action, decisive resolve, upended life. There is no view of learning broadly apace in the north behind Jesus as he proceeded southwards teaching. To the contrary, the texts make a (dramatic) point of "failure in Galilee" and "resolve to go to Jerusalem."

The large picture, painted and not painted, is of lack of learning in response to Jesus' teaching. Overall, people did not learn what he was teaching them.

Select learning

Some people surely did learn. The more focussed picture leaves all other learners aside to look selectively at the disciples and their learning. At first sight the disciples appear as a diffuse, uncircumscribed collection of uncounted and unidentified people about Jesus as he found them here and there. Their response appears positive but unspecific; their learning is uncertain.

With a second look a few dozen individuals come into view--a scribe, a leper, a woman, a Pharisee--and names are given to a dozen or so. These act more clearly and show learning to that extent, then they disappear from view. Some, including the women, continue to be seen clustering around Jesus as helpers and companions as he moves about.

With still more focus twelve named disciples appear and, zooming in, a circle of three comes into view as constant companions of Jesus. They act as agents, helpers, messengers, and foils for his teaching. Their learning too is uncertain. Their depicted responses are of these kinds: lack of understanding; sense of wonder or critical suspicion; persistent disbelief; and opposition to Jesus (Baird, 1969). In summarizing his detailed textual study of their reactions, Baird (1969, p. 36) gives this picture of the twelve select learners.

> Generally speaking, this is not a complimentary picture. The most consistent image is their lack of understanding of most of the major elements of Jesus' mission and message: his meaning and use of parables, the nature of the Kingdom of God, his concept of the *eschaton*, his death and resurrection, his self-conscious identity. They are narrowly Judaistic. They lack faith in him, or in what he teaches, and are constantly amazed, surprised, and afraid of his powers. They do not seem to appreciate him. They are nervously concerned over what the officials are thinking about Jesus and are afraid to antagonize them. They are more interested in the rewards of the Kingdom than in its demands. They are vain, weak, vengeful, constantly at odds with Jesus, either through lack of understanding or downright opposition to his own concept of mission and message.

Few people in the texts are seen fully to respond to Jesus' persuasive teaching (*no one*, according to Robbins, 1984). That includes the select learners to whom Jesus is seen most fully, constantly, and closely teaching by action and word. The three and twelve disciples do not exhibit much learning of that which was being taught to them and before and around them. This most focussed picture actively depicts disciples as not learning.

Lifelong learning

The search for evidence of learning last turns to subsequent developments. The developed picture leaves off from immediate impressions to view the learning as it later matured and manifested itself over the course of life. This view is crucial not only to the case of Jesus but to educational efforts generally. What counts is the learning that students are left with over the long term.

In Graeco-Roman texts of the time, it is a commonplace that discipleship is not expected at the moment of teaching; fulfillment of discipleship is expected to take a lifetime to be seen (Robbins, 1984). In the New Testament texts, this more developed picture is drawn principally by the Acts of the Apostles and the letters of Paul.

This picture can be seen to leave off not only the immediate responses of the disciples but most of the disciples themselves. In their place appear other actors, behind whom can be detected sufficiently large numbers of learners grouped into active communities, developing and manifesting learning with considerable positiveness and intensity. But on the whole, these are *not the people whom Jesus taught* and their learning is *not of his teaching.*

On the one hand, the developed picture clearly shows lifelong learning in response to something and somebody other than Jesus' teaching activity. On the other hand, it fails to reveal the lifelong learning of those whom and that which Jesus did teach.

1. *The Disciples*

The disciples of Jesus, such as they had earlier been seen, make little more subsequent appearance. When seen, they are seen *not* to concern themselves with adopting Jesus' way of living or with preserving his teaching (Conzelmann, 1971). The theme of their community and activity is not their way of life with Jesus and not an effort to realize what they had learned while with him (Schweizer, 1971). For instance, the disciples are not primarily concerned with Jesus' highly critical teaching on law. They neither speak nor act the words or conduct of Jesus in rejecting fasting; to the contrary, they enjoin and practice fasting and other observances of the law. Where Jesus did not baptize, they baptized in Jesus' name; and so on.

More pointedly, the disciples did not teach that which Jesus had taught. Their theme is not the Kingdom of God and repentance but "Jesus," and not Jesus as they had known him. Peter and the other disciples teach not the life and character of Jesus but his death and transfiguration into the Kyrios, Christ Jesus (Acts 3.13, 4.10, 5.30). People learned from this teaching but they were not learning the teaching of Jesus.

Moreover, save for Peter and John, the other disciples are scarcely even depicted. Hence the texts reveal little about the lifelong learning of the disciples. Developed or not, focussed or no, the picture misses them. *Other* figures appear in the foreground and are commonly mistaken as Jesus' disciples.

2. *The Apostles*

Mistaken identity is a major problem with understanding the developed picture of learning. Figures seen later moving about teaching and learning are taken for the figures earlier seen learning with Jesus. "The Twelve Disciples" are taken to be the ones in action, now as "The Twelve Apostles." Having perhaps learned little enough from Jesus at the time, they later develop in learning and go forth to spread his teachings around the globe; through them, millions of people come to learn what Jesus had taught and what his disciples were now passing on to them. This picture contrasts with another which seems rather to be the case.

The case as it developed over time appears at least in outline as follows (reconstructed from Bornkamm, 1971; Schmithals, 1971). Six developments might be distinguished in approximate sequence.

1. During the time that Jesus was teaching, he had disciples, among them twelve named individuals--Peter, John, etc. (Mk 3.15).

2. After Jesus died, he (is depicted to have) appeared to various disciples and gatherings of disciples, principally to Peter and these other eleven named individuals as a group.

3. These twelve individuals then formed the core group of disciples awaiting Jesus' expected imminent return. They were "The Twelve," representatives of the eschatological community, their number in turn representing the twelve tribes of Israel. Not long thereafter the group of "The Twelve" dissolved. (It may have been just before then that one of them, Judas, quit the group or apostatized, "betraying Jesus.")

4a. In the immediately subsequent, apostolic time, these twelve individuals are not seen as group, nor most of them as individuals, nor yet as apostles. They have no activity, no mission trips, no special role in Jerusalem. One of them, Peter, is known as an apostle but not in virtue of being one of "The Twelve," rather for his present teaching or missionary activity. One not of them, Paul, is known as an apostle. Paul knows of "The Twelve" as witnesses to Jesus' post-death appearance, but Paul does not know them in the sense of being acquainted with them; he does not name them, does not see or meet them in Jerusalem, does not speak of or refer to them further. Paul and Peter and other apostles go about teaching about Jesus, and they teach identical things about him (I Cor 15.3-4, 11). Paul makes no effort to teach the life and teaching of Jesus; he does not know what they are, and had never so much as met Jesus in the flesh. He makes a point (Gal 1.16-19) of teaching for three years before going to Jerusalem to meet Peter and James, Jesus' brother, for the first time, "to get information."

4b. In the meantime during the apostolic period, those who are seen and those who are known as apostles are not of "The Twelve," are not of Jesus' disciples, and are not of those who had been taught by Jesus. The exceptions are Peter and John, disciples of Jesus: Peter is of The Twelve and an apostle; John is of The Twelve but not an apostle. The most prominent apostle is James, but not the James of The Twelve. The James of The Twelve is not an apostle; the apostle James is not of The Twelve. He is a blood brother of Jesus but was not a disciple in Jesus' time; he now appears as an apostle and the leading figure in Jerusalem, more prominent than Peter, who had been a disciple and one of The Twelve. Other known apostles not of The

Twelve and not of the disciples during Jesus' lifetime are Barnabas (Acts 15.22; I Cor 9.6), Silas (Acts 15.22; I Thess 2.1+7), Andronicus and Junias (Rom 16.7). Other known actors and teachers are neither disciples nor apostles, for example Apollos (Acts 18.24-28).

5. In the post-apostolic time, when "Luke" came to write the Gospel of Luke and Acts of the Apostles, Paul, once an apostle, is no longer depicted as an apostle, while The Twelve who recently were not apostles are depicted as apostles as well as disciples during Jesus' lifetime, but are not depicted either acting or acting as apostles after Jesus' death.

6. By the turn of the first century AD, "The Twelve Disciples" had become also "The Twelve Apostles" and further *the* apostles, along with Paul (e.g., I Clement 42). In some respect as well, tradition seems to have made of these twelve individuals *the* disciples of Jesus.

Things may not have gone quite this chronological way, but that seems to be the picture as it developed. The developing picture does not show the lifelong learning of Jesus' disciples as it unfolded and manifested itself in subsequent time over the course of life. That which it does depict is either not the disciples but other people, or not the teaching of Jesus but other teaching (about Jesus), or not learning and living what Jesus taught but learning and living something else. It depicts the development and manifestation over life of a learning that is not in response to Jesus' teaching activity, nor a result of it.

The developed picture seems not to reveal evidence of learning from Jesus' teaching. The previously focussed picture appears not to reveal evidence of the disciples' learning what Jesus was teaching them. The diffuse overall picture seems not to reveal evidence of people learning what Jesus was teaching them. The detailed, snapshot picture seems not to reveal evidence of people learning what Jesus was teaching them there and then. A montage of these pictures assembles to *a lack of evidence of learning*, and a permissible inference to *a lack of learning*.

The Answer of Learning

Who learned what from Jesus' teaching activity? There is little evidence of people having learned from his teaching. There is evidence enough that people did not learn what he was teaching them. The learning that subsequently developed was not a result of his teaching activity. Little learning resulted from Jesus' teaching.

As a way of reprising this question and distinguishing the answer proposed here, other answers given to the question will be critically examined. They will be understood in light of the evidence just reviewed and in terms of the question earlier set forth at the start of the chapter.

Assertion of Change

One way of answering the question asserts important learning to have resulted from Jesus' teaching, but provides no evidence of it. For example, "changed lives" is asserted as the "result" of Jesus' teaching, just as "becoming like Jesus" is stipulated as the "purpose" (Magness, 1975). But, this answer continues (p. 634), changed lives cannot be measured, so gauging the result of the education may be impossible.

Whose lives, we may ask, and how many, changed as a result of Jesus' teaching? It is possible to observe "changed lives" even if not to measure them (yet such change can indeed be measured). Where is the evidence of changed lives, wherein did they change, and how did they change in relation to Jesus' teaching activity? For instance, who repented in face of the coming Kingdom of God?

Another example of this approach (Deane, 1922, p. 122) asserts a change in each correspondent as a result of each instance of teaching.

> When the day's teaching was ended and the reluctant crowd dispersed, not one man or woman of them all went away unchanged, either for better or for worse.

How does he know that? one thinks to ask. It seems that a change is being stipulated on some priori ground, evaluated in favor of Jesus (better=accept), and imagined as having happened. At any rate, the gospel texts do not depict many people changing as a result of encountering Jesus, far less every one changing in every instance of teaching.

Case Study

A second approach examines individual cases to assess the learning that resulted. A book subtitled, "the radical impact of Jesus on men of his time" (Smart, 1969) examines the impact in 10 cases of people whom Jesus taught.

Two of the ten are people that Jesus did not teach--John the Baptist and Paul. The others include Peter, Levi, Nicodemus, Judas, Simon the Pharisee, and individuals known not by name but as a theologian or scribe, a Canaanite woman, and a rich man. The rich man is a case of refusal to follow Jesus, rejection of his teaching even in face of a personal appeal to the man, with the result of the man's going away gloomy (Mk 10.22). Judas is known as an apostate. Peter is not known for his learning but for his obduracy and denial of Jesus at a critical moment. But Peter came around later, so he can be counted among the six remaining cases of disciples or positive respondents.

Jesus' impact in these six case studies is assessed principally by tools of imagination and homiletics. The six cases can however well stand on the positive (though not extensive) evidence, yet without instancing "radical impact." Here are six people who learned from Jesus' teaching. How many more cases can be found or detected?

Evidence of Success

A third way of answering the question of learning is to give all manner of evidence of the "success" of Jesus' teaching. The best example is Walter Squires (1927). He is one of the first writers to take the approach and his method and results have been taken up by later writers (e.g., Jones, 1957;

Price, 1946). Squires sets forth evidence from the New Testament and from the passing centuries.

1. *Passing centuries.* These events are problematic as evidence of learning. They include such things as modern democracy, great art, philanthropy, and the millions of Christians around the globe. The latter item is given as a quantitative measure of Jesus' influence (p. 43). These are problematic in that, although traceable in some way to Jesus, they relate uncertainly to his teaching activity, his message and aim, and to the teacher that he was--by contrast to the teaching activity of disciples and apostles about the Christ Jesus. These events do not seem to address the question of the learning that resulted from Jesus' teaching activity.

2. *New Testament.* The events adduced here by Squires are also problematic. They fall into two phases, "immediate effects" and "larger fruitage." There is not much immediate evidence: people called him "teacher," crowds heard him gladly, children were attracted to him, Jesus held the interest of the greatest thinkers of his day. The fact that common people heard Jesus gladly "is evidence of his greatness as a teacher" (p. 41). The larger events occurred after Jesus' death: Peter's great sermon, the Pentecost conversions, the organization of the Christian church, and the beginning of world-wide evangelism. "These are some of the evidences that the teaching of Jesus was efficient" (p. 43). Yet they are not effects of Jesus' teaching activity; they are effects of other things and people. They are not evidences of its efficiency; they are evidences of something else. The subject and aim of Jesus' teaching do not comprehend or portend these events but on the contrary exclude and preclude them--not to mention those cited in the passing centuries.

In missing the question of learning, Squires' detailed answer addresses important related questions such as "the influence of Jesus Christ on world history." Thus this answer serves to clarify the question of learning, rendering it more acute. Who learned what as a result of Jesus' teaching? and, How do we know?

Ends Accomplished

This approach follows the promising method of comparing the aims of Jesus' teaching against the extent of their accomplishment. Learning is evidenced as ends accomplished. John Marquis (1913) is a good example of this approach. As spare and systematic as Squires is prolix and ranging, Marquis is an important example for the originality of the method, the directness with which he pursued it, and the themes that he identified in the course of reporting the results.

Marquis clearly and systematically identifies and compares Jesus' objectives and accomplishments. The four objectives that Marquis had earlier identified for Jesus are later restated for a point-for-point comparison with accomplishments (pp. 48-51).

1. *Impart religious knowledge*: Jesus "left behind him a knowledge of God and his Word no other generation had possessed" (p. 49).

2. *Awaken thought about religion*: "wherever he spoke men began to think as they never thought before" (p. 49).

3. *Induce decision in behalf of religion*: Jesus "brought his hearers to a decision" *but* "only 120 committed themselves to him" *but* "12 of them afterwards turned the world upside down" (p. 49).

4. *Train for service*: that Jesus "was successful in training his disciples for service is patent to every student of the Bible and every reader of history. Those humble fishermen and peasants went out from his class and did what kings could not do" (p. 50).

In this kind of method, much depends on the aims identified as well as the accomplishments described. Only objective #3 fits the aim that Jesus had while teaching. Accomplishments #1 and 2 are suspect, and not only because Jesus did not intend them; irrespective of the teacher's aim, the result of teaching may yet be a deposit of knowledge and widespread thinking. The accomplishments are suspect rather for being apriori evaluations in favor of Jesus--the knowledge is historic and the thinking unprecedented; and for adducing no evidence or demonstration that the result actually happened--that people actually had that knowledge of God and actually did begin to think wherever Jesus spoke. These are claims of learning, made in the first manner of assertion.

The third and fourth accomplishments listed identify important themes about the learning from Jesus' teaching. The third bears directly on the nature, extent, and quality of learning. Here Marquis accurately describes the nature of learning and is one of the few writers to assess extent, to denumerate it, and in so doing to indicate its severe limitation--120 hearers made a positive decision. (Put, however, as a commitment to Jesus rather than to the Kingdom of God.) On this point Marquis is careful to set the smallness of the result against the greatness of the teaching:

> After three years of the best teaching the world has ever heard, during which he spoke to thousands of people, 120 were left, and most of them had to be bolstered up by his post-resurrection ministry. (p. 57)

But then Marquis goes on to reverse the evaluation of this accomplishment by finding that 12 of this small number went on to turn the world upside down. This is the theme of *the few but mighty learners.* They make up for everything by turning local failure into worldwide success, bringing learners in by the millions. A related theme is *the faltering but dazzling learners.* The disciples bumble about uncertainly learning from Jesus, only to reveal themselves later in a display of incalculable learning after he is dead.

The fourth accomplishment follows as a course. Evidence of it need scarcely be given, says Marquis: it is "patent." This is the recurring theme among education writers, that *the learning is self-evident.* What is the evidence? Despite the fact that Jesus did not train the disciples for later service, the disciples may have found themselves trained for service as a result of the teaching. Yet it remains clear that, whatever character and accomplishments the disciples subsequently acquired and displayed, they did not acquire and display these while learning with Jesus; and the character and accomplishment they did acquire and display do not relate to his teaching.

On neither count, then, is that a result of the teaching. It is rather a result of something else.

A recurrent theme behind this accomplishment is that of *the poor material and the magnificent result.* Humble fishermen and peasants outperform kings (Marquis); rustic Galileeans are turned into world-class leaders (Richardson, 1931). "Judged by results," says Marquis, "it is not too much to say that Jesus turned out of his school the greatest generation of teachers the world has ever known" (p. 27). It was nothing for a Plato to result from Socrates, since Plato was a genius; "but to make a teacher of Peter and Thomas and James and their like was an achievement unknown before and unrepeated since" (p. 73). This accomplishment is suspect not only for the fact that Jesus did not intend or provide that these people become teachers; it also represents an a priori evaluation of the result in his favor--the greatest, before or since; it misrepresents the actual result; and it adduces no evidence either of the result itself or of its relation to Jesus' teaching activity.

The twelve disciples may well have gone on to teach, but the only one that can be observed to do so is Peter; while that generation of great teachers observed at work were *not disciples*. Where is the evidence that the other disciples became teachers, became great teachers, or belonged to that signal generation of teachers? Where is the evidence that would link the teaching, and the greatness of it, to Jesus' teaching activity?--to his subject, his aim, his conduct, and the rest? The people that are here pointed to are not the ones exhibiting the purported result, while the thing that is pointed to is not a result of Jesus' teaching.

Tests of learning

A final way of answering the question is best represented by Richardson (1931), one of the most systematic, rigorous, and replete of all education writers on Jesus. Just as Marquis had done, he takes an innovative and systematic approach to determining the learning that resulted from Jesus' teaching.

Richardson's signal merit is to lay repeated stress on evidences, outcomes, and results, and to emphasize looking at the *learners*, not the teacher. "It is what they learn and not, particularly, what the teacher 'teaches,' that counts" (p. 67). He would put this point to the test in a panoply of ways.

> The supreme test...is located in the changes brought about by him in the lives and personalities of his pupils. ...It is one thing to make a direct study of a teacher's technique,...It is quite another matter to study what has happened to his pupils, as a result of their classroom contacts with him, and thus to ascertain his measure of competency as a teacher. (p. 121)

The question of the teacher's competency is here reserved for the next chapter, with the note that Richardson accurately identifies pupil learning as (one) measure.

Emphasizing outcomes and results, Richardson judges Jesus' case "by the results of his teaching. And the place to look for these results is in the experiences of his disciples" (p. 79). Applying this principle to the case of Jesus' learners, Richardson gives a detailed checklist of ten points, "tests of vital learning experiences" (pp. 80-82), then proceeds to evaluate how Jesus' learners meet these criteria (pp. 83-88).

1. Does the knowledge acquired constitute a bond of fellowship among pupils?

2. Do the pupils show a disposition to share with others what they have learned?

3. Do the lessons learned carry over into everyday experience?

4. Do the pupils see a sharp distinction between their lives before and after having studied with the teacher?

5. Do the pupils cherish the memory of their teacher?

6. Are the lessons learned in such a way as to stimulate further learning (study, growth, development)?

7. Are the lessons learned vital, life-giving to pupils?

8. Does what is learned perform the function of truth?

9. Are the pupils intensely interested in what they are trying to learn?

10. Do the pupils welcome opportunities to associate with their teacher?

These ten points are apt ones, and the method is promising. Richardson does not follow in pursuit. Only the first two points are treated in any detail; the remaining eight are treated by the claim that a detailed study "would confirm the conviction that his teaching penetrated to the very center and heart of the personality of each of his disciples" (p. 87). Here again is an answer in the first manner, by assertion.

On the first criterion, *a beloved society of disciples* is instanced "as a direct result of Jesus' teaching" (p. 83). The point is well enough taken. Yet the society pointed to did not form during Jesus' lifetime and did not form as a result of his teaching activity. The society as indicated also embraces such things as the Christian church and Christian democracy, clearly not results of Jesus' teaching.

On the second criterion, Richardson accurately describes *the marvelous faith-propagating urge of Jesus' disciples* (p. 85). That is "evidence of their having learned that which they longed to propagate" (p. 86). But the disciples experienced that urge after Jesus' death, and the urge was exhibited principally by non-disciples. It is indeed evidence of learning, but not of learning that which Jesus taught. Jesus is said to have "deliberately stimulated this impulse to recite to others what one had begun to learn" (p. 86). But this faith-propagating urge could not have been stimulated by Jesus, deliberately or no; for what is in question is the propagation of a faith that Jesus neither possessed nor taught, while the learning that the disciples had begun to acquire and feel the impulse to recite to others was acquired after Jesus' death and recited something that Jesus had not taught.

This latter point plays on the themes of *go tell it on the mountain*, and the *greatest story ever told*. What story was told? Not the story of Jesus but of Christ; not as in the song, that Jesus Christ was born, but that he died and rose from death; not "Repent for the Kingdom of God" but "Believe in Jesus"; and so on. Jesus *did not tell that story or teach that faith*. How can the urge to spread this story and to propagate this faith be held to be learning as a result of Jesus' teaching? That which Jesus taught was not spread; that which was spread was not taught by Jesus.

The Question of Teaching

As far as can be seen, few people learned what Jesus taught. But the answer to the question of learning is not the whole or final response to the question of teaching. Rather it looks to the learner to evaluate the extent and quality of learning. One factor in producing the result is teaching.

The question of teaching looks to the teacher to evaluate the quality of teaching. One factor is the learning that resulted. This factor will again have to be examined, now in other ways, in address to the question of teaching. How good a teacher was Jesus? (chapter 8)

Chapter 8

QUALITY OF TEACHING

Jesus was an accomplished yet ineffective teacher. He taught well, even masterfully in respects, yet the learning that came about did not correspond to the quality of the teaching.

An Assessment of Jesus as Teacher

This assessment answers to two questions which, although commonly confounded, are treated here as independent if interrelated issues--the teacher's competence and effectiveness. How well did Jesus teach? What results did he achieve as a teacher?

Aspects of teaching

How well did Jesus perform the acts of teaching and being a teacher? His overall quality as a teacher may be evaluated by the notion of *congruence* among the different aspects of his teaching, as these are seen in the commonplace categories of teacher, subject and aim, and activity of teaching. Who Jesus was as a teacher, what and why he taught, and how he taught appear to befit one another.

On the other hand, these scarcely befit certain aspects of the milieu and learner categories, where the overall relations describe rather more dissonance than congruence. Yet significant aspects of milieu and learner are not within the province of the teacher and thus fall outside the evaluation of teacher and teaching. For those aspects of milieu and learner that do fall to the teacher, such as use of circumstance to teach, Jesus' teaching seems competent enough, and remarkable in some respects.

Congruence describes the fittingness of the individual aspects of teaching, together with their mutual fit or suitability. To describe these several interrelations will require setting them forth separately one after another, but the notion is that they mutually interrelate and together form a pleasing whole, from a pedagogical perspective.

As detailed in several preceding chapters, Jesus taught in deeds and words, both of them parabolic and actional, in each of which form suited content. Conduct and language of teaching are a congruent pair, as are form and content of conduct and form and content of language; and the three pairs are severally congruent. Singly and together these interrelated aspects of the *activity* of teaching are also congruent with the *substance* of the teaching, itself formed of a congruent pairing of subject-matter and aim. For instance, Jesus' subject-matter consisted of an activity or happening (Kingdom of God) as also did his aim (Repent), the two actional and urgent; as also did and also were the parabolic actions and speech by which he taught them. Action was what he taught, action was how he taught it.

Lack of congruence would be seen, for example, in the teacher's use of didactic exposition and propositional speech to teach the Kingdom of God with the aim that learners memorize information about the impending cosmic upheaval; or to treat the matter and the learning of it as of little enough concern by, for example, a take-it-or-leave-it attitude and a polite analytic discourse. But Jesus' discourse, for instance, was pressing and urgent, immediately and directly addressed to the learner in a second-person, affrontive manner demanding a response in decisive action.

That suggests that the *person* of the teacher also befitted the *substance* and *activity* of the teaching. As a teacher, this person appears to be urgent, demanding, authoritative, impassioned, and single-minded, suitably congruent with the subject-matter and aim of his teaching and the actions and words by which he taught. For the rest, however, this aspect of Jesus' teaching--the person of the teacher--is problematic.

The two primary issues concerning the person of the teacher are: Is he a good person, insofar as a teacher? Is his personality or character appropriate for teaching? These questions cannot readily be answered in

Jesus' case, for two irremovable reasons. First, not enough is known about Jesus' personality and other aspects of his person. Second, the matter is in dispute and the dispute cannot be resolved.

Was Jesus a good person? (as a teacher) The goodness of his person refers to his being virtuous, admirable, attractive, exemplary, and the like whilst *being a teacher*. Further, did he possess goodness of person to such an extent that he can be evaluated as an outstanding or superior teacher? (in this respect of teaching). The point is much disputed, quite apart from the insufficiency of knowledge about his person. It was disputed in his own milieu: he was judged to be an inappropriate person as a teacher, accused as demonic by some and regarded as demented by his family, for and while teaching as he did (and not, for example, for some "private" defect of character in his "personal" life).

Was Jesus' personality appropriate for teaching? Not enough is known of his personality to tell. The few glimpses seen of it in his actions and words reveal scattered good points and scattered bad points. Despite today's touchiness and cautiousness about making personality judgments, including personality evaluations in a teacher's personnel file, people have a sense of the kind of person they want to be teachers and they know the particular traits, in some number, that are unarguably desirable and undesirable for teachers to exhibit. Jesus exhibited not enough of the desirable traits and too many of the alarmingly undesirable ones to see him through a year's tenure in any school, even through an employment interview. In his own milieu, moreover, his personality (e.g., his attitudes towards religious observance) struck many learners the wrong way, and professionals (e.g., Scribes) publicly judged him unsuited to be a teacher. His personality repelled as well as attracted various people whom he taught.

Whatever the acceptableness of his person and personality, the assessment cannot be made that Jesus as a teacher was possessed of sufficient goodness of person and appropriateness of personality such as to make him a superior or even a good teacher, in this respect of teaching. Not enough is known of him in these personal respects; and that which is known of him is not good enough.

That is not to say that Jesus was *not* a good person; he may well have been, the point is and was disputed but present ignorance makes it moot. That is not to say that he was not a good person as a teacher; this point too is and was disputed but present knowledge is enough to preclude a judgment as to his superior quality in this respect.

In other respects there is no hesitation in judging Jesus a good teacher. On multiple detailed accounts his performance of the acts of teaching is masterly. On the overall account, moreover, the congruence among all aspects of his teaching describes such fit and befittingness as to qualify him as a superior teacher. No one need agree with the teaching to see that it is for this reason a demonstration of pedagogical accomplishment of the first rank.

How well did Jesus teach? This is a question of competence. He taught well. What results did he achieve as a teacher? This is a question of effectiveness.

Effects of teaching

As far as can be known, Jesus had little effect as a teacher. His personality had little effect, his subject-matter had little effect, his methods had little effect. Great effects were observed to follow, but not in the manner of after-effects. Rather they are effects of something else--some other personality, subject-matter, and methods.

This answer to "How effective was Jesus as a teacher?" distinguishes between the factor of Jesus and other factors, and between the lifetime of Jesus and later times. On these distinctions three questions arise. What is the effect of Jesus' teaching (1) during his lifetime, and (2) over subsequent time? (3) To which factors other than Jesus' teaching may subsequent effects be traced? These questions and their answers are schematically exhibited in Table 15.

Table 15 exhibits three commonplaces of teaching--personality, substance, activity; identifies the placeholders for each category during two time periods--Jesus' lifetime and thereafter; and draws relations between

Table 15 - Effects of Jesus' Teaching, and Sources of Other Effects

CATEGORY OF TEACHING	JESUS' LIFETIME	APOSTOLIC TIMES TO PRESENT TIME
PERSONALITY OF TEACHER	Jesus of Nazareth ---> little effect (ca. 4BC-30AD)	(1) Jesus Christ ----> GREAT EFFECT (2) Jesus the Exemplar ----> Some Effect
SUBSTANCE OF TEACHING (a) thematic teaching	"The Kingdom of God ---> little effect is near! Repent!"	"Jesus Christ lives, saves, & returns! ----> GREAT EFFECT Believe in Christ Jesus!
(b) other teachings	selected points ----> little effect	(1) from Jesus ----> Mixed Effect (2) about Jesus (3) about other things ----> Some Effect
ACTIVITY OF TEACHING	methods of Jesus ----> little effect	(1) methods of Apostles (2) methods of Christian Church ----> GREAT EFFECT

factors and effects for each placeholder in the three categories during the two time periods. These relations are drawn as a result of two complementary analytic activities: identifying the effects of the Jesus factors; and identifying the factors for other effects. These various factors and effects are commonly confounded, while others commonly remain unidentified. Of primary concern here are the effects of Jesus as a teacher. Details of the other effects are of little concern, save to note that these effects are due to some other factors.

1. *Personality*

In the category of person (Table 15) there is Jesus of Nazareth. The personality and other characteristics of this teacher had little positive effect on his contemporaries. Some people were attracted to the person of this teacher and otherwise responded positively to this personality; most were not, and responded negatively.

The great effect observed over subsequent times describes the widespread positive response accorded another personage in the same category--"Jesus Christ the Lord and Savior," the *kyrios christos* proclaimed by apostles after Jesus' death. It is to this person that people responded; whereas people did not on the whole respond to Jesus of Nazareth the teacher, neither then nor later, nor to anywhere near the extent and intensity of response to Jesus the Christ. The gospels and other New Testament texts make it plain--it is their paradigmatic point--that the person at hand is Jesus Christ, a transfiguration of the person of Jesus of Nazareth.

Some later effect is also observed of yet another person, Jesus the Exemplar. Numbers of people who do not respond to the personage of Jesus Christ find in the Jesus of the gospels a person who was a good man, lived a good life, taught admirable ideals, and so on, leading them to hold him worthy of imitation in some respect, interesting to contemplate, and deserving of a place among other outstanding human exemplars and/or teachers of humankind. In that way, for example, Jesus appears with Socrates, Buddha, and Confucius as "the paradigmatic individuals" in the first volume of *The Great Philosophers* (Jaspers, 1962).

The two figures of Jesus the Savior and Exemplar are related in some obscure way to the teacher Jesus of Nazareth. Both figures are mediated by the gospel texts, in both cases rendered more clearly than the figure of the Nazarene teacher in whose life and person the texts are plainly little interested. But they clearly are not the same person as the latter, nor do people who respond to the one think themselves responding to the other.

In either event, the great effect subsequently produced and observed is due not to the person or personality of the teacher Jesus of Nazareth but to some other personage or personality image. The personality of Jesus the teacher had comparatively little effect.

2. *Substance*

In the category of substance of the teaching (Table 15), there is Jesus' thematic teaching of "Kingdom of God, Repent!" together with scattered other teachings, e.g., sayings in closer and remoter relation to that theme.

His thematic teaching or message had little effect. Some few people accepted it and acted accordingly; most rejected or ignored it. It is a matter of fact, not passing unnoted at the time, that the Kingdom of God did not come and that people did not repent. The non-arrival of the Kingdom provoked in Jesus' followers agitation during his lifetime, consternation at his death, and perplexity for a time thereafter. They did not take up this theme nor did they continue teaching it. They taught something else.

The great effect in subsequent times is due not to Jesus' thematic teaching--*that subject was dropped*--but to another teaching of which *Jesus* is the theme; and the theme is not Jesus himself, so to speak, but the aforementioned personage into which he was transfigured, now to become the subject of teaching and the object of belief rather than knowledge. This theme runs something like: "Jesus Christ lives, saves, and will return! Believe in Christ Jesus!"; and other such formulas taught by disciples, apostles, and successive missionaries, preachers, and churchmen.

The other, non-thematic, teachings of Jesus of Nazareth had no more effect than his thematic teaching had but even less, for they would have been taken up principally if not solely as part of accepting and acting upon the teaching of the Kingdom. In that character they are scattered teachings, side points, illustrations, selected matters and the like; and that is how they have been preserved, among numerous others lost and further ones added on. In subsequent times these also form part of the non-thematic substance of later teaching, selected points from Jesus that are taught by others. These have no great effect but a mixed effect. Some of the points are selected, taught, and accepted ("learned"). Others are accepted by some people and rejected by others. Still others are never selected for teaching in the first place but are rejected by being explained away or just ignored.

For all the rest, those teachings of Jesus preserved as they are in the gospel texts served from the beginning and continue to serve as objects of liturgy, ritual, apologetics, and devotion. Selected points among them are permissibly taken up--though others are expressly forbidden--by individuals who so wish, as for example, to live in accordance with them. But they are not enjoined among his followers. They particularly do not serve as objects of belief: Jesus' teachings figure in the Christian canon but *not in the creed.* (They are not so much as mentioned in the "The Apostles' Creed" and the like.) The objects of belief are teachings about Jesus. These are the teachings that produced such great effect.

Some effect is also observed for other selected points about Jesus and about all manner of other things (theology, ethics, etc.). These have some effect but are not teachings of Jesus. The thematic teaching has great effect but is not the teaching of Jesus.

In any event, the observed effects are due not to the teachings of Jesus but to other teachings which are not things that Jesus taught. The things that Jesus taught were not subsequently taken up and taught but ended with his teaching activity. The teachings of Jesus had comparatively little effect.

3. *Activity*

In this category (Table 15) are the teaching methods of Jesus, the activity by which he went about teaching the things that he taught. Jesus' teaching methods had little effect. Some people learned from them, most people did not; some learned from a given activity, others did not.

The great effect subsequently observed is due in the first place to the teaching activity of the apostles and thereafter of the Christian church. The apostles and churchmen notably do not take up, continue, or even use the methods whereby Jesus taught. They use a different method of teaching, and appropriately so; for, their subject matter and aim are not those of Jesus but a teaching about Jesus and many other things, and not about the person who was Jesus the teacher but the person who is Jesus Christ the Lord and Savior. Their method of teaching was phenomenally effective. The great effects are due to their teaching activity, not to that of Jesus. The teaching activity of Jesus had comparatively little effect.

How effective a teacher was Jesus? As far as can be seen, he was not very effective. How competent a teacher was Jesus? That is, how well did he teach? He taught well. The result was good teaching. Good learning is another matter, resulting from a complex of conditions one among which, and an indirect one, is good teaching. In Jesus' case the quality of learning did not match the quality of teaching. That is the common case with other teachers too.

To evaluate Jesus or others as teacher is to assess the quality of teaching. But if learning is to be the criterion, and teachers are to be judged by "results" or effectiveness, then Jesus must be assessed as a remarkably poor teacher, no matter how well he taught.

Other Assessments

No assessment in the educational literature concludes to any failure or imperfection of Jesus as a teacher. To the contrary, he is seen as exemplary in every respect and he is evaluated in the highest possible terms: perfect on every count. These assessments will be reviewed by first reciting their terms of praise, next by examining their approaches to the task of assessment, and lastly by noting their conclusions about various aspects of Jesus as a teacher.

Encomia

Terms of the very highest praise are used, always in the superlative, in assessing Jesus as a teacher. Moreover, in his case the term teacher is customarily given a capital T, with the superlative adjective also capitalized, as in "The Master Teacher." Four superlatives are commonly used by writers early and recent as an overall assessment.

1. *The Perfect Teacher.* (Coleman, 1964; Kealy, 1977; Stevens, 1901). For example: "a perfect Teacher. He never made a mistake" (Coleman, 1964, p. 17).

2. *The Great Teacher.* (Boyden, 1930; Hill, 1905; Hughes, 1932; Perkins, 1929; Stein, 1978).

3. *The Master Teacher.* This is the title of Horne's (1920) book and a phrase frequently used since (Barclay, 1960; Bennion, 1981; Bernetta, 1939; Jones, 1957; Price, 1946; Richardson, 1931; Stemple, 1961; Wilson, 1974).

4. *The Greatest Teacher Ever.*
   - "history's greatest" (Bauman, 1960);
   - "of all time" (Conrad, 1945; Rixon, 1977);
   - "this world has ever known" (Deane, 1922; Squires, 1927);
   - "the world's greatest" (Shafto, 1923).

The placement of these terms in the published text enhances their character as encomia, showing them to be not casual remarks but principled positions or thematic judgments of Jesus as a teacher. "The Great Teacher" figures as the title of articles (Boyden, 1930; Hughes, 1932; Perkins, 1929) and as the title of the first section in the article (Boyden, 1930). "The Master Teacher" forms the title of books early and late (Bennion, 1981; Horne, 1920); the title of the first chapter (Richardson,

1931) and later chapters (Barclay, 1960); the very first sentence of the book and the first sentence of every chapter therein (Jones, 1957).

Approaches to Assessment

How are these judgments arrived at? What method of assessment is followed to come to these terms of highest evaluation of Jesus as a teacher?

1. *Self-evidence*

There is first the denial of method, a position holding that the greatness of Jesus as a teacher is *self-evident* (McKoy, 1930; Squires, 1927; Rixon, 1977). This approach implies that prior to any systematic evaluation the evaluative conclusion had already been arrived at by some unknown means, perhaps by stipulation or revelation. For example:

> A study of the teaching methods of Jesus yields no surprises and no disappointments. As a Teacher he is all that we imagined, and more; and doubtless it will continue to be said about Him...that He is the greatest Teacher of all time. (Rixon, 1977, p. 8)

By being placed at the head of the study, this axiomatic position is not reporting a conclusion that will follow from later considerations and that is only being foreshadowed in the introduction; it announces the principle that the study must have begun with, even before the outset. The clearest statement of it is given by Squires (1927) at the start of his chapter on "The Incomparable Teacher" (p. 37):

> Jesus has been called the incomparable teacher of all the ages. That he is such is evident to an informed and candid mind. The presentation of evidence concerning the matchless power of Jesus as a teacher is hardly necessary to convince the readers of this book that he is the greatest teacher the world has ever known.

From this basis, authors proceed to present further considerations that illustrate this first principle, rather than providing the materials from the examining of which a principled judgment can be derived. That is, the remainder of the book will illustrate rather than demonstrate Jesus' greatness as a teacher. It is in that way that the study can yield "no surprises and no disappointments," for it presents only the case that it begins with.

2. *Apriori argument*

The next consideration to be advanced is therefore an *apriori argument*. In its short and clearest form, the argument holds that every aspect of Jesus as a teacher is superlative *because* he is a superlative teacher. Chapter after chapter argues, for example, that "His teacher-pupil relationships were ideal, for He was the Master Teacher" (Wilson, 1974, p. 86). The more common form argues from Jesus' divinity to his perfection as a teacher. What is "the final secret of his marvelous power as a teacher"?--"his divine personality" (Piper, 1931, p. 106). What is "the source of his matchless teaching"?--"a divine teacher presenting a divine message by divinely-discerned methods" (Roberts, 1955, p. 5).

The logic of this argument was fully set forth, perhaps unwittingly so, by Squires (1927). It may be schematized as follows.

I. "The presentation of evidence is not necessary" (p. 37).

II. A. "Christians have long believed in the faultless personality of Jesus.

B. "They have likewise insisted upon the faultless character of his teachings.

C. 1. "If he was perfect in his personality and if he taught a perfect system of truth, it is only logical to assume that he was perfect in the methods of teaching which he employed" (p. 47).

2. "Since Jesus was a faultless teacher his teaching methods must have been in harmony with sound educational principles" (p. 63).

III. "In our effort to discover the secret of Jesus' greatness as a teacher we have found plausible explanations in his matchless personality, in the universality and enduring truth of his message, in his faultless methods and in the principles on which these methods rested" (pp. 49-50).

Thus the secret is discovered after having been proclaimed from the start. With this position announced at the outset and established by apriori argument in Chapter 2, the remaining 250 pages of Squires' book have only to provide illustrative details and to withhold non-illustrative ones. The non-illustrative details are not ignored, nor reprehensibly withheld, for by force of following this method the investigator will never have encountered or noticed them in the first place.

3. *Analysis of categories*

A third approach to assessing Jesus as a teacher is to establish *categories of teaching* and to evaluate Jesus' case within each category--ideally after having described and examined the case. What did Jesus do with respect to aspect X of teaching, and aspects Y and Z? How well did he do them? The categories most commonly treated form a trinity of teacher personality, message, and method, in each aspect of which Jesus is evaluated as perfection itself (Boyden, 1930; McKoy, 1930; Roberts, 1955; Squires, 1927; Stein, 1978).

As indicated, this trinity is most commonly treated by introducing the divinity of Jesus and concluding to his perfection as a teacher. For their being divine or perfect, therefore, Jesus' personality as a teacher is matchless, unique; his message of teaching is universal and true; his method of teaching is faultless, unequaled in skill. The three categories form not a triplet but a "tri-unity" in Jesus' case, rendering it "the loftiest pinnacle of great teaching," one that "cannot fail of success" (McKoy, 1930, p. 154). For that very reason of cannot-fail, perhaps, the conclusion must follow: "That Jesus was successful is self-evident" (p. 168).

4. *List of items*

A variation of this approach is taken by less systematic authors who make *lists of items* that reveal the high quality of Jesus' teaching. There are four reasons that make him a great teacher: loftiness of standards, exemplariness of life, intensity of love, and soundness of method (Perkins, 1929). There are six or ten elements that made him effective or great--such as his use of parables or proverbs (Barclay, 1960; Bennion, 1981).

The longest and most varied list, by Horne (1920, pp. 202-203) itemizes Jesus' five qualifications as a world-class teacher, plus seven others that make him history's greatest teacher. He is a world-class teacher for having a world-view, knowledge of his subject-matter, and of his pupils, aptness at teaching, and an imitable character. Beyond these items, his followers outnumber those of any other teacher, and nations that are Christian lead the world's civilization. Further, Jesus taught the solution of man's greatest problems, together with the highest moral and spiritual truths; he taught these truths simply and effectively, from the highest motives, and he committed them to a few people whom he trained as witnesses. These thirteen items flit in and out of various categories, including personality, message, method, touching here and there on most of the evaluative affirmations that have been made by others since Horne dressed his list. Two of the items have been adopted and extended by later writers in a kind of aposteriori argument, forming yet another approach to assessment.

5. *Aposteriori argument*

The *aposteriori argument* concludes from subsequent events to Jesus' greatness as a teacher. Horne (1920) had neatly made this argument by setting forth two brief considerations, quantitative and qualitative (as he called them).

The quantitative consideration was succinctly made by citing statistics of membership in the world's various religions. One-third of the earth's population was Christian in 1920, a greater proportion than for any other religion. "As a simple quantitative fact, Jesus is today the world's greatest teacher" (p. 201).

The qualitative point was made by affirming that nations bearing Jesus' name (by which is meant *Christ's* name, or Christian) lead the world's civilization. Therefore, "Jesus, judged by quantitative and qualitative results, is the world's greatest teacher" (p. 201).

This pointed rendering of the argument was taken up by later authors who repeated Horne's demographic and cultural citations as well as his conclusion, and who enhanced the argument by extending the qualitative, cultural consideration. Later, the 1971 edition of Horne's book supplied updated statistics, thereby enhancing also the demographic point to show Jesus to be an even greater teacher today than he was in 1920. If in the year 2020 plague, famine, or war decimate the Christian population but not the Buddhist, Jesus will become less of a teacher than he was even in 1920, and Buddha greater.

Horne's cultural, qualitative argument has been stretched to its limit. Squires (1927) affirmed that Jesus' influence was felt in every department of life, citing government, art, and philanthropy. Later Jones (1957) cited several other fields, affirming that Jesus' teaching stopped foot-binding in China, cannibalism in Africa, and infanticide in India (p. 147). The point was most fulsomely argued by Price (1946), who detailed eight categories of life influenced by Jesus' teaching (pp. 122-135). These are said to be due to Jesus' teaching.

1. *Personality exalted.* For example, Jesus' teaching resulted in female suffrage and officeholding.

2. *Lives transformed.* Not only Peter, James, John and the rest at the time but also Augustine, Abelard, Luther and the remainder down to Wesley and Moody in modern times.

3. *Reforms stimulated.* Jesus' teachings brought about the great moral reforms of history: emancipation of women; rights of children; racial equity; The Reformation; abolishment of slavery; and the U.S. law of Prohibition against alcohol.

4. *Institutions improved.* In addition to home and marriage, the growth of modern democracy is due to Jesus' teaching, as are schemes for management- and profit-sharing in industry and labor.

5. *Literature permeated.* Jesus is more frequently quoted in books than any other writer who ever lived, and is salient as well in poetry, theology, ethics, history, psychology, and sociology.

6. *Arts influenced.* These include music, painting, architecture, and motion pictures.

7. *Philanthropy inspired.* Due to Jesus' teachings are not only the hospitals, orphanages, and nursing homes but also academies and colleges, as well as the monies donated by Carnegie and Rockefeller whose consciences were disturbed by Jesus' teaching.

8. *Service motivated.* The Red Cross gets its motive from the teaching of Jesus, not to mention Livingston and Jane Addams.

These are the events subsequent to Jesus and unrelated to his teaching that are called "results" of his teaching and which are adduced as quantitative and qualitative considerations for the aposteriori argument that Jesus is the world's greatest teacher.

6. *Criteria of teaching*

A last approach to assessment establishes *criteria of teaching* and then examines the extent to which Jesus' case meets the set criteria. On both counts this is a formidable task. Only glimpses of it may be seen in the literature, and only in a few smaller studies (Boyden, 1930; Hinsdale, 1895; Marquis, 1913; Shouse, 1955), with the signal exception of Richardson's (1931) book-length study where the approach is followed in its most systematic and developed form.

The very first sentence of Richardson's book, the first sentence of his first chapter entitled "Jesus, the Master Teacher," sets forth the program. (Here the sentence will be set off by phrases.)

> A study of Jesus Christ's mastery, as a teacher, may be made,
>
> first, by noting the chief characteristics of competency in teaching, as defined by the science of education, and,
>
> second, by a careful analysis of his manner of teaching, viewed from the standpoint of these scientific criteria. (p. 3)

Richardson identifies five criteria and summarizes his later analysis of Jesus' case for each. It so happens that the five items also represent five major categories of teaching, which here will be added to Richardson's scheme.

1. In the category of AIM or PURPOSE of teaching, Richardson's criterion is *clear objectives*. Jesus had "definitely formulated 'learning outcomes'" which were clear: "righteousness of conduct" (p. 59).

2. SUBJECT - *mastery of subject-matter*. Jesus had "amazing knowledge of his subject," profound and comprehensive (p. 23).

3. In the category of TEACHER or of LEARNER, the unqualified criterion is *relations with pupils*. Jesus showed "self-sacrifice and devotion" towards pupils (p. 24).

4. METHOD - *skill in technique.* Jesus had "amazing skill" and "mastery of the technique of teaching" (p. 26). He was versatile, showing "startling originality and effectiveness" (p. 140). Later Richardson cites three dozen aspects of Jesus' technique.

5. TEACHER - *a personality that demonstrates the teaching.* Jesus' personality was "God-centered" and "he lived what he taught" (p. 28).

In addition to this "five-fold competency," Jesus is also shown to exhibit seven principles of creative teaching and to pass ten tests of student learning. The latter point introduces the category of result of teaching, and leads to the judgment that Jesus was an effective as well as competent teacher (e.g., p. 180).

Conclusions of Assessments

The conclusions that education authors draw from their studies, or draw their studies from, evaluate the personality of Jesus, his pedagogy, and his success as a teacher. (These are not the conclusions of this present study but of other studies.)

1. *Personality*

The personality of Jesus as a teacher receives the highest praise, as does everything else about him and his teaching. Some authors start and end their evaluation of the teacher's person by affirming that he was divine (Conrad, 1945; Roberts, 1955; Russell, 1944); the remainder say that he was perfect. This perfection of personality is cited as the key or secret to his success or greatness as a teacher (e.g., Boyden, 1930; Piper, 1931; Roberts, 1955; Squires, 1927).

Detailed personality profiles of Jesus have commonly been displayed to make this point, usually in the form of listings of personality or character traits. All manner of desirable traits, and no undesirable one, are found in him, and found to a pronounced degree. Jesus is rated, for example (Shouse, 1955, pp. 151-152), as highly intelligent, well-informed, exceedingly sensitive; a good leader and a good mixer; industrious, courageous, confident and optimistic. He shows intellectual acumen, mastery of situations, and democracy of spirit; intensity, sincerity, and humility; gentleness, joyousness, and altruism (McKoy, 1930, pp. 36-41). He possesses power, knowledge, command, poise, patience, devotion, persistence, fearlessness and earnestness (Smith, 1916, pp. 16-28). Not mentioned or perhaps noticed are Jesus' display of brusqueness, severity, vituperation, exasperation, inflexibility, distemper, violence, and the like. Disregarded or unavailable to psychological sensitivity is the fragmented and inconsistent portrait of the person of the teacher in the gospels, rendering impossible any personality profile whatsoever save by tools of imaginative construction.

In final evaluation of Jesus' person as a teacher, most authors observe that Jesus *personified* his own teaching: his person exemplified his message (e.g., Horne, 1920; McKoy, 1930; Richardson, 1931; Russell, 1944). This summative trait is widely and emphatically cited as the reason for Jesus' perfection and greatness as a teacher (Bennion, 1981; Hubery, 1970; Kealy, 1978; Perkins, 1929; Roberts, 1955). Moreover, it is said to make him unique among all other teachers (Shouse, 1955; Stein, 1978).

2. *Pedagogy*

Jesus receives equally high praise for his use of methods and principles of teaching. Education writers lay understandably greater emphasis on this aspect of the teacher, and treat it in finer evaluative detail. That follows from the nature of the book or article, for education authors typically choose as their task the treatment of Jesus' methods of teaching; other aspects of Jesus as a teacher (e.g., his subject matter, his personality) receive briefer treatment.

These evaluations may be summarized as the mastery, multiplicity, and modernity of Jesus' methods and principles of teaching.

Mastery. As with the personality of the teacher, Jesus' mastery of teaching methods is assessed as perfect where not divine. The methods he used are faultless and the principles at least sound (McKoy, 1930; Perkins, 1929; Squires, 1927; Stein, 1978; Stemple, 1961). His skill with techniques of teaching is amazing, consummate, rare, unequalled (Boyden, 1930; Hinsdale, 1895; McKoy, 1930; Richardson, 1931). Moreover, his use of dialectic and questioning is rated as more skillful than that of Socrates himself, who is noted to be the founder and hitherto the purportedly most accomplished practitioner of the art (Horne, 1920; Montague, 1884; Singleton, 1977; Squires, 1927).

Multiplicity. The multiplicity of Jesus' methods and principles shows his versatility as well as mastery of teaching. For example, in one single episode of teaching, Jesus' encounter with "the woman at the well" (Jn 4.5-41), no fewer than sixteen pedagogical principles are discerned at work (Horne, 1920), as well as various methods and techniques, including Jesus' use of programmed instruction (Wilson, 1974). Nineteen methods in all, listed in Table 16, have been discovered in Jesus' teaching activity.

The many methods listed in Table 16 are not a sum of those identified by various authors; each author specifies a multiplicity of methods. Of the dozen authors cited, all specify 7 or 8 methods, and a few 17 or 18, for an average of nine methods each. The average number of principles discerned to underlie Jesus' methods is six. Thus Jesus is uniformly evaluated as demonstrating mastery of a multiplicity of teaching methods and principles. That is to make of Jesus' every *geste* and syllable a method of teaching, under each of which there may be espied a principle of education.

Modernity. Furthermore, these methods and principles are seen to be modern, as the case of programmed instruction and team-teaching (Table 16) might suggest. Not only did Jesus exhibit all the methods and principles of today, he also set their standard for the future, anticipating the whole of modern educational science (Gilmary, 1962; Horne, 1920; Perkins, 1929; Piper, 1931; Price, 1946; Raven, 1929; Smith, 1916). The modern educational expert is only adopting the methods and principles of Jesus the Master Teacher (Deane, 1922) who two thousand years ago was already putting into practice the slogans of modern scientific pedagogy (Perkins, 1929). "And the wonder of it all is that these principles were so skillfully employed in a time when the knowledge of man on the subjects of

Table 16. Characterizations of Jesus' Teaching Methods*

METHOD	EXAMPLE	METHOD	EXAMPLE
A. DIDACTIC METHODS		C. ACTIVITY METHODS	
1. Lecture	Mt 5-7	12. Visual Aids/object lesson	Mt. 18.1-4
2. Textbooks (Scriptures)	Mk 7.5-13	13. Drama, dramatics	Mt 21.12-16
		14. Demonstration	Mt 11.2-19
3. Storytelling (parables, narratives)	Lk 10.25	15. Project/laboratory	Mt 10.1-42
4. Illustration	Lk 14.28-33	16. Topical research	Mt 11.2-6
5. Repetition	(parallel sayings)		
6. Silence	Mt 15.23		
B. INTERACTIVE METHODS		D. OTHER METHODS	
7. Conversation	Jn 3.1-21	17. Examinations	Jn 6.5-7
8. Discussion	Jn 13.31-14.31	18. Programmed instruction	Jn 4.5-41
9. Forum	Mt 22	19. Team teaching	Mt 5-7
10. Question-answer	Mt 17.25-26		
11. Panel (question-answer in reverse)	Jn 6.25-66		

*source: Hinsdale, 1895; Horne, 1920, Hubery, 1970; Jones, 1957; Marquis, 1916; McKoy, 1930; Piper, 1931; Price, 1946; Rixon, 1977; Roberts, 1955; Squires, 1927; Tipsword, 1916, Wilson, 1974 (each source citing 7-8 to 17-18 methods).

pedagogy and psychology was extremely limited" (McKoy, 1930, p. 108). No wonder that Jesus is thought to be the world's greatest teacher.

These latter appreciations have rightly been charged with the intellectual errors of modernization or anachronism (Kealy, 1978; Weigle, 1939).

3. *Success*

Jesus' success as a teacher is evaluated in terms commensurate with the divinity or perfection of his personality and the mastery and multiplicity of teaching methods and principles. Success refers to his achievement of learning in his contemporaries and his enduring influence over populations and activities around the present world. These describe not merely his competence as a teacher but above all and essentially his effectiveness. What results did he achieve?

Nothing is more obvious than the thought that a good teacher makes students learn. Only on second thought does that whole notion collapse in confusion, for the absurdity of the idea that learning has for its agent and cause teaching; and with it collapses the question of what results the teacher achieved. No reflection stalls the thought of education writers who assess Jesus as a teacher. Their universal appreciation of him praises his teaching for effectively achieving profound learning and perduring influence.

This chapter and the previous one have extensively discussed the issue of results in learning and influence. It remains to be noted that Jesus' claimed but unobserved success with his disciples and subsequent others is attributed to the perfection of his teaching, whereas his observed but unclaimed failure with Pharisees and other contemporaries is attributed to imperfections of the learner. This evaluative stance is most clearly shown in one of the most systematic and sophisticated of the educational sources, the book-length study by Richardson (1931).

Richardson spends pages in praising Jesus' varied teaching skill in making learners of disciples in spite of every possible obstacle and "learning difficulty," especially in the disciples' personalities and social relationships. He cites Jesus' "astonishing achievement and superior effectiveness" in teaching, case for case, people who were misinformed, who lacked understanding, who possessed false attitudes, and who needed supervised practice (p. 180). They learned because of Jesus' teaching.

But the Pharisees and others of that ilk, says Richardson, did not learn because they did not have "the learning attitude," and because they exhibited various other difficulties such as prejudice. "It is not surprising to find that Jesus Christ, great teacher though he was, made little headway in an educational task where conditions were as unfavorable as this" (p. 190).

Yet, taking Richardson's same evaluative principle and none other, the permissible correlations between teaching and learning are in (1) below rather than (2).

(1) Either (a) The learning is the teacher's success and the non-learning is the teacher's failure;

or (b) The learning is the learner's success and the non-learning is the learner's failure.

(2) Either (a) The learning is the teacher's success and the non-learning is the learner's failure;

or (b) The learning is the learner's success and the non-learning is the teacher's failure.

Principle (2a) informs Richardson's evaluation of Jesus as a teacher, as it does, less systematically, the assessments by all other education writers. Plainly enough, none of the cited principles (1) or (2) is defensible. Teacher and learner together participate in the activity and its outcome, and success and failure has to be carefully evaluated for the two together, not to mention for the two as they are implicated and influenced by other aspects of teaching such as subject matter, aim, and especially milieu.

In that way, for example, students of a competent teacher may still not learn; and the evaluator need not insist that a good teacher *must* also prove to be effective. In Jesus' case, however, it seems to be stipulated in advance that the teacher be both superlatively competent and overwhelmingly effective, that the results of his teaching must be commensurate with the quality of the teaching; such that there must be astonishing learning from his amazing teaching, even with the poor material of disciples--except of course in the case of the Pharisees, when the amazing teaching does not come into question because of the poor learning material.

Any assessment of a case of teaching has to account, in *the same terms*, for both positive and negative results. Apriori stipulations do not yield a consistent and persuasive account. Jesus can be a competent teacher without also being an effective one. If not, then the assessment is called upon to explain why a perfect or divine personality having mastery over a multiplicity of teaching methods and achieving the profoundest results in learning and enduring influence in the most disparate and unpromising cases, should, in the case of a few Pharisees or many ordinary Jews,--what? (*fail*?).

Such an account needs to be given in complement to the account of *Jesus' success* in making character over--turning the impulsive and unsteady into the steady and dependable, hothead into lovable, persecutor into promoter, money-grubber into philanthropist (Price, 1946); in preparing poor peasants and fishermen to outperform kings (Marquis, 1913); and in transforming rustic Galileeans into cosmopolitan leaders (Richardson, 1931). What, in these *same terms*, of the decent, hard-working, law-abiding and God-fearing Pharisees? What, in these same terms, of the dusty-footed pedestrians--peasants and fishermen, rustic Galileeans too--who walked away from his teaching?

If the first case is attributed to Jesus' extraordinary teaching and evaluated as his success, then the evaluator must assess the second case as his failure. There proved to be a handful of the first case and a majority of the second. The evaluative conclusion is nonetheless universally drawn that Jesus was an outstandingly effective and successful teacher.

SUMMARY ASSESSMENT

Jesus cannot be shown to be a successful and effective teacher. He was nonetheless a demonstrably good one.

Appendix

THE STUDY OF JESUS AS A TEACHER

How may we understand Jesus as a teacher? This general problem is answered chapter by chapter in the book, which reports a case study of the famous historical teacher, Jesus of Nazareth. Each chapter takes up one main aspect of Jesus' teaching, asks one main question about that, and forms an answer by examining the case of Jesus from the viewpoint of several disciplines and fields of study.

The understanding that results depends upon the approach taken to study--for example, the methods used. And this understanding can be compared to the conclusions of other studies on the same topic. This Appendix describes the approaches taken in studying this problem here, then it surveys other studies over the past century.

Approach to Study

The approach or method followed here studies Jesus the teacher by identifying common categories of teaching and by examining his case in each category, as seen through the light of various scholarly disciplines. It is a multidisciplinary case study of all aspects of Jesus as a teacher.

Categories & questions for study

Categories are devices used to understand some domain or subject by classifying it into different important aspects that together make up the whole. What are the different things that must be taken into account when trying to understand the domain of teaching?--so as to understand the case of Jesus' teaching.

There is first of all the *teacher*, then the *learner*, and the *subject* taught and learned. Teacher and learner engage in some *activity* over that subject, with some *aim* in view and with some *result* as an outcome. All of this occurs in a given time and place, in some circumstance or *milieu*. These are the seven categories of teaching used in this study. To understand teaching is to understand <u>teacher and learner interacting over subject-matter in circumstance towards an intended result in learning</u>.

Categories are particularly useful devices for understanding for the further reason that they correlate with questions: there is one generic question for each category (and any number of specific questions that are variants of the generic question). Answering this question is the way to understand the kind of thing in that category. This study asks seven questions about Jesus as a teacher, one each in the seven categories of teaching.

1. *Teacher* - Who was Jesus?

2. *Learner* - Whom did Jesus teach?

3. *Subject* - What did Jesus teach?

4. *Milieu* - Where and when did Jesus teach?

5. *Aim* - To what end did Jesus teach?

6. *Activity* - How did Jesus go about teaching?

7. *Result* - Who learned what from the teaching?

Taken together, the answers to these questions describe Jesus as a teacher. A final question is then asked to evaluate his *quality* as a teacher. How good a teacher was Jesus? or, How well did he teach? These questions and answers are given chapter by chapter in this book, forming an understanding of Jesus as a teacher.

Fields & disciplines of study

These questions about Jesus are answered here from a multidisciplinary perspective, so as to come to a satisfying understanding of Jesus as a teacher--an understanding that is comprehensive and reliable, representing all and the best knowledge available. It still remains *an* understanding; and the understanding proposed in this book may still not satisfy. How good this understanding is depends on, among other things, two factors. Ultimately it depends on the uses to which the understanding can successfully be put. But in the first place it depends on the methods used to answer the questions about Jesus as a teacher. The multidisciplinary approach of this study relies on the perspectives and findings contributed by various scholarly disciplines pursued in two broad fields: New Testament, and Education.

The field of New Testament studies concentrates on a collection of short texts about Jesus and the very beginning of Christianity, commonly entitled *New Testament*. Scholars in this field examine these texts from one or another disciplinary perspective, such as history and linguistics; that is, some New Testament scholars are historians, others are linguists. Some few are accomplished theologians as well as being historians or linguists; but most scholars are only historians, or only linguists, interested in these particular texts rather than (or in addition to) other ancient texts.

Altogether, New Testament studies contribute a range of knowledge about Jesus as studied by history and archaeology, linguistics and philology, theology, rhetoric, and literary theory. For example, they have minutely examined, from every possible angle, the language used by Jesus.

Education is a field of practice, to the understanding of which various scholarly disciplines are brought to bear. For example, psychologists may study the teaching-learning process and philosophers the aims of education. Thus there are in this field "educational psychologists"; and there are also researchers from "pure" psychology who choose to study the problems that interest them (e.g., learning, thinking) in the context of a school rather than in some other context.

Altogether, educational research contributes a range of knowledge about teaching, as studied by psychology and philosophy, history, sociology and anthropology, and some aspects of linguistics (e.g., socio-linguistics).

Both of these fields are plainly needed to understand the case of Jesus as a teacher. Either field without the other yields knowledge that is unsatisfying for being either partial or uninformed. Put crudely, New Testament scholars know about Jesus but not about teaching; educational researchers know teaching but not Jesus. Hence it happens that conclusions about Jesus as a *teacher*, stated by a New Testament scholar, sound odd to an educational researcher, whose own conclusions about *Jesus* as a teacher sound odd to a New Testament scholar. Each knows something that the other doesn't.

Knowledge from all of these disciplines in both fields helps to form a satisfying understanding, by formulating answers to the questions about the subject of this study, Jesus the teacher, as he is represented in the sources.

Subject & sources of study

The subject of study is the figure of the historical teacher called Jesus of Nazareth. Little enough is known of this figure by contrast to the transcendent personage of Jesus Christ, or Jesus the Lord and Savior, who in turn is a transfiguration of the historical individual, the teacher Jesus of Nazareth, the subject of study here.

The principal sources for knowing about Jesus of Nazareth are the collected texts of the *New Testament*. Anyone may read these texts and form an understanding of this teacher. But as with any process of reading, and especially with reading any ancient text, the understanding depends greatly on the sophistication of the reading process and of the reader's knowledge of the text *as* a text.

The principal texts about Jesus are called the *gospels*, and these are named as Mark, Luke, and Matthew (abbreviated in the book as Mk, Lk, Mt), as in "The Gospel of Mark" or "according to Mark." Together these are termed the synoptic gospels, or the synoptics, for the fact that much of the one is contained in the other, the three having had some lost sources in common. The convention is to refer to these texts by chapter and verse, such that, for example, the fifth line or verse in the eighth division or chapter of Mark's gospel is cited as: Mk 8.5 (or 8:5). These same numberings also appear in the text as printed in any edition of the *New Testament*.

A fourth gospel, by John, also appears in the New Testament canon but is not used as a source for this study, for the fact that it is not regarded as a reliable source of historical information about Jesus. (There also exist other gospels not in the New Testament canon, also not used as sources here.) John's gospel is a theological and mystical rendering of Jesus, to an extent markedly greater than the synoptics. Nonetheless, references to John appear in this book (as Jn) when certain points are at issue, most frequently as part of reviewing the work of other scholars whose conclusions are based on John and whose references to him are therefore cited in this book.

The synoptic gospels used here as sources (Mark, Luke, Matthew) are quite short, together filling about 200 smallish pages of text. Mark is the shortest and oldest. They were composed and written a generation or more after Jesus' death. To appreciate the nature of these texts requires actually reading them, for the gospels form of themselves a unique literary *genre*--that is, a type of literature of which no other instances exist. They are not biographies of Jesus or records of his teaching. They are artfully composed and edited collections of disparate types of selected material--sayings, events, dialogues, tableaux, stories, commentary, etc.--rendering an impression of Jesus for one and another purpose--apologetics, liturgy, devotion, confession of faith, etc.

Some of the elements of which the gospels are composed represent subsequent written forms of an originally oral tradition, as for example, sayings of Jesus either remembered of him or attributed to him. Lists of these, no longer extant, came to be made and circulated for various purposes, none biographical or documentary. One or another item from one or another list was selected and worked into one or another gospel. That is one example of one of the ways that one part of the gospel material came to be written down in the form in which we now have it. Further, the original manuscripts or copies are no longer extant, while some of the texts are Greek, Syriac, or

Coptic translations of the original Aramaic which Jesus spoke and in which his sayings were circulated in the earlier oral and written traditions.

In short, the gospels are at some remove from the original event. Moreover, that fact is of no concern to the gospel writers nor to the people for whom the gospels were written. They were not interested in the subject of this study, the teacher Jesus of Nazareth, nor were they interested in studying him. They were interested in some other personage and purpose, related in some obscure way to the man who went about teaching in Palestine around the year 30 A.D. Almost everyone who today reads the gospels is also interested in that other personage and purpose.

Two other kinds of New Testament texts also serve as sources for this study. A single text called "Acts of the Apostles," written by the same individual who wrote "The Gospel of Luke," represents the activities of some of those who went about teaching about Jesus in the years just after his death (from about 30 to 65 A.D.). A few "Letters" by one of these earliest teachers or apostles, Paul, are the oldest texts of all to be written and provide one or two informative details relating to Jesus as a teacher. These letters are known by their recipients, who were communities of Christians in Galatia, Corinth, and Thessalonia (abbreviated as Gal, Cor, Thess). There are other letters by Paul in the New Testament, letters by others than Paul, and texts other than letters and gospels and the one "Acts." These are not used as sources here.

Such are the principal textual sources for knowledge about Jesus the teacher, primarily the three synoptic gospels of Mark, Luke, and Matthew. To construct from them an understanding of Jesus the teacher, these texts are read with the help of the perspectives and findings of multiple disciplines of inquiry from two fields, New Testament studies and Education, in search of answers to seven interrelated questions about seven kinds of things that together describe teaching. That is the approach taken here to study the case of Jesus as a teacher.

A Century of Study

Studies of Jesus as a teacher, conducted from a specifically educational viewpoint, have appeared throughout the last one hundred years, since the establishment of "education" as a field of scientific or scholarly research. (It has always been a field of practice.) As a convenient summary, Table 17 lists the available studies (in English) decade by decade. They are also listed in the bibliography of this book, along with other studies from Education and all the New Testament studies consulted. In that way an interested reader can gain a sense of the century of study of Jesus as a teacher.

Table 17 lists six dozen books, chapters and journal articles published on Jesus as a teacher, together with a few university theses or dissertation studies. It is important as well as useful to identify and gather all of these into one place, such as in Table 17, because no one seems to know that this literature exists.

It is as if this body of literature or tradition of study did not exist, and that is regrettable for constraining our knowledge. Very few of the authors in Table 17 base their studies on previous studies. Most of the authors do not even refer to previous studies. Many of the authors even state that previous studies have never been done.

Across the whole century, various authors have prefaced their own study with the statement that little or nothing had previously been done to study Jesus' teaching from a specifically educational point of view. Near the beginning, in 1902, the famous psychologist and educator, G. Stanley Hall, thought that Ellis' study of Jesus' method of teaching was new and unique for its purely pedagogical viewpoint (introduction to Ellis, 1902, p. 391); and so he published it in his journal, *Pedagogical Seminary & Journal of Genetic Psychology*. And in that year Griffith-Jones (1902) thought it surprising that so few writers had dealt with Jesus' method of teaching; hence his book on that subject. Justly so, for in 1905 Hill discovered in a bibliography of 3200 books in the somewhat new field of educational research only four that related to Jesus.

But in 1916 Tipsword's book was introduced, just as Ellis' 1902 study had been, as new and unique for studying the pedagogy of Jesus--no other writer had done so, states the foreword (Tipsword, 1916, p. xv). By that time Griffith-Jones' earlier book had already appeared in its third edition (1914), not to mention a half-dozen other books--see Table 17. Nonetheless in 1928 an author stated that no serious attempt had previously been made to study Jesus' way of teaching (Raven, 1928).

Thereafter authors regularly repeated, decade after decade, the same surprise that Griffith-Jones had registered in 1902: surprisingly little written (Jones, 1957), surprisingly little attention (Hubery, 1970), surprisingly few books (Wilson, 1974), amazing neglect, nothing to date on Jesus' technique of teaching (Kealy, 1978). "Some such study is surely long overdue," it was averred (by Hubery, 1970, p. 5), after several dozen such studies had already been published over the preceding 70 or 80 years.

One of the recent authors (Wilson, 1974), surprised like the others over the few books on Jesus' teaching method, took care to list a few available ones in his bibliography, since this was originally his advanced university thesis. After listing Horne's 1971 book *The Teaching Techniques of Jesus*, he notes that Horne had also written *Jesus, The Master Teacher*, in 1920. Even though the renowned professor of education Horne had died decades before 1971, the book was not posthumously published; it is a verbatim reprint, from the same plates, though under a different title, of his 1920 book. (Another book to cite Horne, McKoy 1930, was also originally a dissertation, done under Horne's supervision.)

This critical review is made in favor of establishing a tradition of study of Jesus as a teacher, by at very least identifying the available literature. Then new efforts to study Jesus can be situated within a recognized tradition and a consulted literature; studies can be compared, criticized, and used for the lessons and knowledge they might offer to the new investigation. Some of the earliest studies are quite useful; some of the more recent ones are not.

With a few exceptions, all of the studies in Table 17 are fascinating to read, not only because of a reader's interest in the topic but also to see the various methods and approaches taken to study Jesus as teacher, the knowledge proposed in conclusion, and the various purposes for undertaking the study and proposing the knowledge. All of these may be put to some serviceable use. For example, some of these books are by professors and other scholars in education, religious education, or divinity; some are by practitioners. Some books are systematic and principled, others are inspirational and devotional, and others are handbooks for group discussion or practical guidance of teachers. Some of the unassuming little practical books are better studies than some of the scholarly works. That sounds less paradoxical when it is realized that knowledge in education is of a practical as well as theoretical kind.

The uses made of these studies in the present study may be put generally as taking them into account. For example, their conclusions are reviewed or otherwise cited for the various issues and questions studied here; and they are compared, usually critically, against the conclusions of this study. On almost every point but one or two, the present study diverges from previous studies; they are not cited in support of present conclusions. In part the conclusions diverge because of different methods and purposes of study; in other part they diverge because of changing knowledge from research in Education and New Testament fields. For example, recent knowledge about Jesus' language was not available to earlier writers.

The final use made of these studies is to identify them as forming an existing yet unknown literature, and a neglected but possible tradition of study, setting them out for interested readers and future scholars to consult. It may be that each generation needs to construe for itself Jesus as a teacher, in order to come to its own satisfying understanding.

This book describes one such effort within a century of study. Its conclusions differ strikingly from all other studies, and uncomfortably so. The conclusions here may not satisfy overall, and may even strike oddly here and there. But that is the way they work out, given constraints of method and limitations of knowledge about Jesus and about teaching. The book proposes what this study has been brought to conclude as being the most reliable answer that can presently be given to the question, How may we understand Jesus as a teacher?

Table 17. A Century of Study of Jesus as a Teacher

BOOKS & Chapters		ARTICLES (& Theses)
	1880's & 1890's	
Wendt, *The Teaching of Jesus* (chapter)		Montague, "The Dialectic Method of Jesus"
Bruce, *The Training of the Twelve* (1st ed. 1871)		
Hinsdale, *Jesus as a Teacher*		
	1900's	
Stevens, *The Teaching of Jesus* (chapter)		*Ellis, "The Pedagogy of Jesus"
Burrell, *The Wonderful Teacher, and What He Taught*		*Hill, "Jesus Christ: The Educator"
*Griffith-Jones, *The Master and His Method*		
Ross, *The Teaching of Jesus* (chapter)		
	1910's	
Marquis, *Learning to Teach from the Master Teacher*		Van Wagnen, "The Pedagogy of Jesus"
Sedgwick, *Christ the Teacher*		
Smith, *Jesus--Teacher*		
*Tipsword, *The Pedagogics of Jesus*		
Rall, *The Teachings of Jesus*		

Table 17. A Century of Study of Jesus as a Teacher (continued)

BOOKS & Chapters	ARTICLES (& Theses)
1920's	
Horne, *Jesus--The Master Teacher* (reissued 1971)	*Raven, "The Teaching Method of Jesus"
Deane, *Rabboni: A Study of Jesus Christ the Teacher*	Raven, "The Teaching Method of Jesus and That of Today"
Shafto, *The School of Jesus* (3rd ed.)	Perkins, "The Great Teacher"
Squires, *The Pedagogy of Jesus in the Twilight of To-day*	
Raven, *Christ and Modern Education*	
1930's	
McKoy, *The Art of Jesus as a Teacher*	Boyden, "Teaching as the Greatest Teacher Taught"
Manson, *The Teaching of Jesus*	Frank, "Jesus as a Teacher"
Piper, *How Would Jesus Teach?*	Hughes, "The Great Teacher"
Richardson, *The Christ of the Classroom*	Bernetta, "Our Lord, The Master Teacher"
Baldwin, *Asked and Answered: Queries and Inquiries Addressed to and by the Lord Jesus Christ by and of His Contemporaries*	
Wiegle, *Jesus and the Educational Method*	
1940's	
Curtis, *Jesus Christ the Teacher*	Goodier, "Jesus, the Teacher"
Russell, *Jesus the Divine Teacher*	Conrad, "Jesus the Divine Teacher"
Price, *Jesus the Teacher*	

Table 17. A Century of Study of Jesus as a Teacher (continued)

BOOKS & Chapters		ARTICLES (& Theses)
	1950's	
Lafferty, *Impressive Queries: A Study of Questions by Christ, to Christ, about Christ in the Gospels and Acts*		Raymond, "Effect of the Dialectic upon our View of Christ as Teacher"
*Jones, *The Teaching Methods of the Master*		Sorensen, "How Christ Used Questions" (thesis)
		Roberts, "The Teaching Methods of Jesus Christ"
		Shouse, "Jesus as Teacher"
	1960's	
Bauman, *The Life and Teaching of Jesus* (chapter)		Stemple, "Qualities of the 'Master Teacher'"
Barclay, *The Mind of Jesus* (chapter)		Gilmary, "Christ and Modern Method"
Coleman, *The Master Plan of Evangelism*		
Colman, *The Master Teachers and the Art of Teaching* (chapter)		
	1970's	
*Hubery, *The Teaching Methods of Jesus*		Magness, "Teaching and Learning in the Gospels"
Horne, *The Teaching Techniques of Jesus* (reissue of 1920 book)		Kealy, "Jesus the Unqualified Teacher"
*Wilson, Clifford, *Jesus: The Master Teacher*		Singleton, "The Lord's Use of Questions in Matthew" (thesis)
Wilson, Carl, *With Christ in the School of Disciple Building: A Study of Christ's Method of Building Disciples*		Crow, "Teaching and Motivating: The Jesus Model"
Rixon, *How Jesus Taught*		
Pogue, *Questions Jesus Asked*		

Table 17. A Century of Study of Jesus as a Teacher (continued)

BOOKS & Chapters		ARTICLES (& Theses)
	1970's (continued)	
Hilton, *Questions Jesus Wouldn't Answer ..?*		
Grassi, *Jesus as Teacher*		
*Kealy, *Jesus the Teacher*		
Stein, *The Method and Message of Jesus' Teachings*		
	1980's	
		Dillon, "The Effectiveness of Jesus as a Teacher"
Alfonso, *How Jesus Taught*		Dillon, "The Questions and Dialogues of Jesus"
Bennion, *Jesus the Master Teacher*		Dillon, "The Historical Character of Jesus and its pedagogic Uses"
*Delnay, *Teach as He Taught*		
Robbins, *Jesus the Teacher*		Giles, "Teachers and Teaching in the Church"
		Grassi, "The Gnostic View of Jesus and the Teacher Today"
	1990's	
Dillon, *Jesus as a Teacher*		

*authors stating that little or nothing has previously been written on Jesus as teacher.

BIBLIOGRAPHY

Alfonso, Regina (1986). *How Jesus taught*. Staten Island, NY: Alba.

Amiot, Francois, Brunot, A., Danielou, J., & Daniel-Rops, H. (1962). *The sources for the life of Christ*. New York: Hawthorn.

Anderson, Hugh (Ed.) (1967). *Jesus (Great Lives Observed)*. Englewood Cliffs, NJ: Prentice-Hall.

Aulen, Gustaf (1976). *Jesus in contemporary historical research*. Philadelphia: Fortress.

Aune, David E. (1980). *Jesus and the synoptic gospels: A bibliographic study guide*. Madison, WI: Inter-Varsity.

Ausubel, David (1963). *The psychology of meaningful verbal learning*. New York: Grune & Stratton.

Baird, Joseph A. (1969). *Audience criticism and the historical Jesus*. Philadelphia: Westminster.

Baldwin, Harry Anderson (1938). *Asked and answered: Queries and inquiries addressed to and by the Lord Jesus Christ by and of his contemporaries*. New York: Revell.

Bammel, Ernst & Moule, C. F. D. (Eds.) (1984). *Jesus and the politics of his day*. Cambridge: Cambridge University Press.

Barclay, William (1960). *The mind of Jesus*. New York: Harper & Row.

Barrett, Charles K. (1970). *The signs of an apostle*. London, Epworth.

Bauman, Edward W. (1960). *The life and teachings of Jesus*. Philadelphia: Westminster.

Bellack. Arno A., Kliebard, H. M., Hyman, R. T., & Smith, F. L. (1966). *The language of the classroom*. New York: Teachers College.

Bennion, Lowell L. (1981). *Jesus the master teacher*. Salt Lake City, UT: Deseret Book Company.

Bernetta, Sister Mary (1939). Our Lord, the master teacher. *Catholic School Journal*, 39, 249-250.

Betz, Hans D. (1979). *Galatians*. Philadelphia: Fortress.

Black, Matthew (1967). *An Aramaic approach to the gospels and Acts* (3rd ed.) Oxford: Clarendon Press.

Blinzler, Josef (1971). Jesus and his disciples. In Hans Jurgen Schultz (Ed.), *Jesus in his time*, pp. 84-95. London, SPCK.

Bloom, Benjamin S. (Ed.) (1956). *Taxonomy of educational objectives. Handbook I: Cognitive domain*. New York: McKay.

Bornkamm, Gunther (1960). *Jesus of Nazareth*. New York: Harper & Row.

Bornkamm, Gunther (1971). *Paul*. New York: Harper & Row.

Bornkamm, Gunther (1974). Jesus Christ. *The New Encyclopedia Britannica* (15th ed.), Vol. 10, pp. 145-155.

Bouquet, A. C. (1953). *Everyday life in New Testament times*. New York: Scribner.

Boyden, Arthur C. (1930). Teaching as the greatest teacher taught. *Journal of Education*, 111, 364-366, 394-395, 420-421, 423, 475-476, 506, 508, 534-535 (6-part article).

Braun, Herbert (1979). *Jesus of Nazareth: The man and his time*. Philadelphia: Fortress.

Brown, Colin (Ed.) (1976). *History, criticism, and faith*. Leicester: Inter-Varsity Press.

Bruce, Alexander B. (1894). *The training of the twelve* (4th ed. rev.). New York: Armstrong.

Bultmann, Rudolf (1958). *Jesus and the word* (rev. ed.). New York: Scribner. (1st ed., 1934)

Bultmann, Rudolf (1968). *The history of the synoptic tradition*. (3rd ed.). New York: Harper & Row.

Burgess, Harold W. (1975). *An invitation to religious education*. Notre Dame: Religious Education Press.

Burney, Charles F. (1925). *The poetry of our Lord: An examination of the formal elements of Hebrew poetry in the discourses of Jesus Christ.* Oxford: Clarendon Press.

Burrell, David James (1902). *The wonderful teacher, and what he taught.* New York: Revell.

Burrows, Millar (1977). *Jesus in the first three gospels.* Nashville: Abingdon.

Catchpole, David R. (1984). The "triumphal" entry. In Ernst Bammel & C. F. D. Moule (Eds.), *Jesus and the politics of his day*, pp. 319-334. Cambridge: Cambridge University Press.

Coleman, Robert E. (1964). *The master plan of evangelism* (2nd ed.). Old Tappan, NJ: Revell.

Colman, John E. (1967). *The master teachers and the art of teaching.* New York: Pitman. Chapter 6, "The Parable Method," pp.44-50.

Conrad, Simon (1945). Jesus the divine teacher. *Catholic Educational Review*, 43, 94-100.

Conzelmann, Hans (1971). The influence of Jesus after his death. In Hans Jurgen Schultz (Ed.), *Jesus in his time,* pp. 142-148. London: SPCK.

Conzelmann, Hans (1973). *Jesus.* Philadelphia: Fortress.

Cornfeld, Gaalyah (1982). *The historical Jesus: A scholarly view of the man and his world.* New York: Macmillan.

Crossan, John Dominic (1973). *In parables: The challenge of the historical Jesus.* New York: Harper & Row.

Crossan, John Dominic (1993). *The historical Jesus.* San Francisco: Harper.

Crossan, John Dominic (1994). *Jesus: A biographical portrait.* San Francisco: Harper.

Crow, Porter J. (1978). Teaching and motivating: The Jesus model. *Momentum*, 9 (2), 10-15.

Curtis, William A. (1943). *Jesus Christ the teacher: A study of his method and message based mainly on the earlier gospels.* London: Oxford University Press.

Dalman, Gustaf H. (1902). *The words of Jesus*. Edinburgh: T. & T. Clark.

Dalman, Gustaf H. (1929). *Jesus-Jeshua: Studies in the gospels*. London: SPCK. (New York: KTAV reprint, 1971).

Daniel-Rops, Henri (1962). *Daily life in the time of Jesus*. New York: Hawthorn.

Deane, Anthony C. (ca. 1922). *Rabboni: A study of Jesus Christ the teacher*. London: Hodder & Stoughton, n.d.

Delnay, Robert G. (1987). *Teach as he taught*. Chicago: Moody.

Dibelius, Martin (1949). *Jesus*. Philadelphia: Westminster.

Dillon, J. T. (1981a). The effectiveness of Jesus as a teacher. *Lumen Vitae*, 36, 135-162.

Dillon, J. T. (1981b), The questions and dialogues of Jesus. *Living Light*, 18, 199-215.

Dillon, J. T. (1982). The historical character of Jesus and its pedagogic uses. *Journal of Christian Education*, 73, 44-51.

Dillon, J. T. (1988). *Questioning and teaching*. New York: Teachers College.

Dillon, J. T. (1990). *Personal teaching*. Lanham, MD: University Press of America.

Dillon, J. T. (1994). *Using discussion in classrooms*. Buckingham, England: Open University Press.

Dodd, Charles, H. (1970). *The founder of Christianity*. London: Macmillan.

Dolto, Francoise, & Severin, Gerard (1979). *The Jesus of psychoanalysis: A Freudian interpretation of the gospel*. Garden City, NY: Doubleday.

Ellis, E. E. (1980). Dating the New Testament. *New Testament Studies*, 26, 487-502.

Ellis, G. Harold (1902). The pedagogy of Jesus. *Pedagogical Seminary (Journal of Genetic Psychology)*, 9, 441-459.

Fitzmyer, Joseph A. (1979). *A wandering Aramean: Collected Aramaic essays.* Missoula, MT: Scholars Press. (SBL Monograph Series No. 25)

Flusser, David (1969). Jesus in the context of history. In Arnold Toynbee (Ed.), *The crucible of Christianity: Judaism, Hellenism, and the historical background to the Christian faith.* New York: World Publishing Co.

France, R. T. (1976). The authenticy of the sayings of Jesus. In Colin Brown (Ed.), *History, criticism, and faith*, pp. 101-141. Leicester: Inter-Varsity Press.

Frank, Glenn (1930). Jesus as a teacher. *High School Teacher*, 6, 49-50 & 82.

Fuchs, Ernst (1964). *Studies of the historical Jesus.* London: SCM. (Studies in Biblical Theology No. 42)

Funk, Robert (Ed.) (1994). *The five gospels.* New York: Macmillan.

Giles, Kevin N. (1981). Teachers and teaching in the church, I and II. *Journal of Christian Education*, papers 70 (April), 5-17 and Papers 71 (July), 52-62.

Gilmary, Sister (1962). Christ and modern method. *Catholic School Journal*, 62, 49.

Goodier, Floyd T. (1943). Jesus, the teacher. *School and Society*, 57, 225-230.

Goodspeed, Edgar J. (1957). *The twelve: The story of Christ's apostles.* Philadelphia: Winston.

Grant, Michael (1977). *Jesus: An historian's review of the gospels.* New York: Scribner.

Grassi, Joseph A. (1978). *Jesus as teacher: A New Testament guide to learning "The Way."* Winona, MN: St. Mary's College Press.

Grassi, Joseph A. (1982). The Gnostic view of Jesus and the teacher today. *Religious Education*, 77, 336-349.

Griffith-Jones, Ebenezer (1902). *The master and his method.* London: Hodder & Stoughton. (3rd ed., 1914).

Groome, Thomas H. (1980). *Christian religious education: Sharing our story and vision.* San Francisco: Harper & Row.

Guignebert, Charles (1956). *Jesus*. New York: University Books. (originally published in 1935).

Hahn, Ferdinand, Lohff, W., & Bornkamm, G. (1969). *What can we know about Jesus*? Philadelphia: Fortress Press.

Harrow, Anita H. (1972). *A taxonomy of the psychomotor domain*. New York: McKay.

Hengel, Martin (1977). *Crucifixion*. Philadelphia: Fortress.

Hill, Mabel (1905). Jesus Christ: The educator. *Education*, 25, 285-291.

Hilton, Donald H. (1977). *Questions Jesus wouldn't answer..?* Nutfield, England: Denholm House.

Hinsdale, Burke A. (1895). *Jesus as a teacher, and the making of the New Testament*. St. Louis: Christian Publishing Company.

Horne, Herman H. (1920). *Jesus--The master teacher*. New York: Association Press. (reissued as *Teaching techniques of Jesus*. Grand Rapids, MI: Kregel, 1971).

Hubery, Douglas S. (1970). *The teaching methods of Jesus*. London: Chester House.

Hughes, Erwin H. (1932). The great teacher. *National Education Association Proceedings*, 70, 33-39.

Hughes, Philip E. (1974). The languages spoken by Jesus. In Richard N. Longenecker & Merill C. Tenney (Eds.), *New dimensions in New Testament study*, pp. 127-143. Grand Rapids, MI: Zondervan.

Hultgren, Arland J. (1979). *Jesus and his adversaries: The form and function of the conflict stories in the synoptic tradition*. Minneapolis: Augsburg.

Humphreys, Colin J. & Waddington, W. G. (1983). Dating the crucifixion. *Nature*, 306, 743-746 (22/29 December).

Jaspers, Karl (1962). *Socrates, Buddha, Confucius, Jesus: The paradigmatic individuals*. (*The Great Philosophers*, vol. I). New York: Harcourt, Brace & World.

Jeremias, Joachim (1963). *The parables of Jesus* (rev. ed.). New York: Scribner.

Jeremias, Joachim (1966). *Rediscovering the parables.* New York: Scribner. (easier version of Jeremias, 1963).

Jeremias, Joachim (1971). *New Testament theology: The proclamation of Jesus.* New York: Scribner.

Jeremias, Joachim (1971). *The problem of the historical Jesus.* (Biblical Series No. 13). Philadelphia: Fortress Press.

John Paul II (1979). *Catechesi tradendae.* Vatican: Vatican Polyglot Press.

Jones, A. H. M. (1938). *The Herods of Judea.* Oxford: Clarendon Press.

Jones, Claude C. (1957). *The teaching methods of the master.* St. Louis; Bethany Press.

Joyce, Bruce & Weil, Marsha (1992). *Models of teaching* (4th ed.). Boston: Allyn & Bacon.

Kealy, Sean P. (1977). Jesus the unqualified teacher. *African Ecclesiastical Review*, 19 (4), 228-233.

Kealy, Sean P. (1978). *Jesus the teacher.* Denville, N.J: Dimension Books.

Kissinger, Warren S. (1985). *The lives of Jesus: A history and bibliography.* New York: Garland Publishing Company.

Krathwohl, David R., & Bloom, Benjamin, & Masia, Bertram (1964). *Taxonomy of educational objectives. Handbook II: Affective domain.* New York: McKay.

Kummel, Werner G. (1961). *Promise and fulfillment: The eschatological message of Jesus* (3rd ed. rev.). London: SCM. (Studies in Biblical Theology No. 23)

Lafferty, John P. (1956). *Impressive queries: A study of questions by Christ, to Christ, about Christ in the gospels and Acts..* New York: Exposition Press.

Leaney, A. R. C. (1966). Historicity in the gospels. In Anthony Hanson (Ed.), *Vindications: Essays on the historical basis of Christianity*, pp. 103-134. London: SCM.

Lee, James Michael (1985). *The content of religious instruction: A social science approach*. Birmingham, AL: Religious Education Press.

Longenecker, Richard N. & Tenney, Merrill C. (Eds.) (1974). *New dimensions in New Testament study*. Grand Rapids, MI: Zondervan.

Mager, Robert F. (1962). *Preparing instructional objectives*. San Francisco: Fearon.

Magness, Lee (1975). Teaching and learning in the gospels: The biblical basis of Christian education. *Religious Education*, 70, 629-635.

Manson, Thomas W. (1935). *The teaching of Jesus: Studies of its form and content* (2nd ed.). Cambridge: Cambridge University Press.

Marquis, John A. (1913). *Learning to teach from the master teacher*. Philadelphia, PA: Westminster.

Marshall, I. Howard (1977). *I believe in the historical Jesus*. Grand Rapids, MI: Eerdmans.

Martin, Ralph (1977). Approaches to New Testament exegesis. In I. Howard Marshall (Ed.), *New Testament interpretation: Essays on principles and methods*, pp. 220-251. Grand Rapids, MI: Eerdmans.

Merkel, Helmut (1984). The opposition between Jesus and Judaism. In Ernst Bammel & C. F. D. Moule (Eds.), *Jesus and the politics of his day*, pp. 129-144. Cambridge: Cambridge University Press.

McKoy, Charles F. (1930). *The art of Jesus as a teacher*. Philadelphia: Judson.

Montague, Richard (1884). The dialectic method of Jesus. *Bibliotheca Sacra*, 41, 549-572.

Moule, C. F. D. (1967). *The phenomenon of the New Testament*. (Studies in Biblical Theology, Second Series, No. 1). London: SCM.

National Conference of Catholic Bishops (1972). *To teach as Jesus did: A pastoral message on Catholic education.* Washington, DC: U. S. Catholic Conference.

Perkins, Everett V. (1929). The great teacher. *Education*, 50, 229-232.

Perrin, Norman (1967). *Rediscovering the teaching of Jesus.* New York: Harper & Row.

Perrin, Norman (1976). *Jesus and the language of the Kingdom: Symbol and metaphor in New Testament interpretation.* Philadelphia: Fortress Press.

Piper, David R. (1931). *How would Jesus teach*? Elgin, IL: Cook.

Pogue, V. C. (1974). *Questions Jesus asked.* Edinburgh: Church of Scotland Department of Education.

Preston, R. H. (1966). Ethical criticisms of Jesus. In Anthony Hanson (Ed.), *Vindications: Essays on the historical basis of Christianity*, pp. 135-152. London: SCM.

Price, J. M. (1946). *Jesus the teacher.* Nashville, TN: Southern Baptist Convention.

Rall, Harris F. (1918). *The teachings of Jesus.* New York: Abingdon Press.

Raven, Charles E. (1928). The teaching method of Jesus. *International Review of Missions*, 17, 577-587.

Raven, Charles E. (1929). The teaching method of Jesus and that of today. *International Review of Missions*, 18, 47-58.

Raven, Charles E. (1929). *Christ and modern education.* New York: Holt.

Raymond, S. (1950). Effect of the dialectic upon our view of Christ as teacher. *Catholic Educational Review*. 48, 596-605.

Reicke, Bo (1971). Galilee and Judea. In Hans J. Schultz (Ed.), *Jesus in his time*, pp. 28-35. London: SPCK.

Richardson, Norman E. (1931). *The Christ of the classroom.* New York: Macmillan.

Rixon, Lilas D. (1977). *How Jesus taught.* Croydon, Australia: Sidney Bible College.

Robbins, Vernon K. (1984). *Jesus the teacher: A socio-rhetorical interpretation of Mark.* Philadelphia: Fortress.

Roberts, Francis H. (1955). *The teaching methods of Jesus Christ.* Unpublished Th.M. thesis, Dallas Theological Seminary.

Robinson, James M. (1959). *A new quest of the historical Jesus.* (Studies in Biblical Theology No. 25). London: SCM.

Ross, D. M. (1904). *The teaching of Jesus.* Edinburgh: T. & T. Clark. (reprinted 1926)

Russell, William (1944). *Jesus the divine teacher.* New York: Kenedy.

Sabourin, Leopold (1972). Hellenistic and rabbinic 'miracles.' *Biblical Theology Bulletin*, #3, 281-307.

Schalit, Abraham (1969). Palestine under the Seleucids and Romans. In Arnold Toynbee (Ed.), *The crucible of Christianity: Judaism, Hellenism, and the historical background to the Christian faith.* New York: World Publishing Company.

Schalit, Abraham (1971). Herod and his successors. In Hans J. Schultz (ed.), *Jesus in his time*, pp.37-46. London: SPCK.

Schillebeeckx, Edward (1979). *Jesus: An experiment in Christology.* New York: Seabury.

Schmithals, Walter (1971). *The office of apostle in the early church.* London: SPCK.

Schultz, Hans Jurgen (Ed.) (1971). *Jesus in his time.* London: SPCK.

Schwab, Joseph J. (1971). The Practical: Arts of eclectic. *School Review*, 79, 433-442.

Schwab, Joseph J. (1973). The practical: Translation into curriculum. *School Review*, 81, 501-522.

Schway, Joseph J. (1983). The practical 4. *Curriculum Inquiry*, 1983, 13, 239-265.

Schweizer, Eduard (1971). *Jesus*. London: SCM.

Sedgwick, W. M. (1919). *Christ the teacher*. London: Student Christian Movement.

Shafto, G. R. H. (1923). *The school of Jesus: A primer of discipleship* (3rd ed.). London: Student Christian Movement.

Sherwin-White, A. N. (1963). *Roman society and Roman law in the New Testament*. Oxford: Oxford University Press.

Shouse, J. B. (1955). Jesus as teacher. *Educational Forum*, 19, 150-157.

Singleton, Robert C. (1977). *The Lord's use of questions in Matthew*. Unpublished Th.M. thesis, Dallas Theological Seminary.

Sloyan, Gerald S. (1964). Catechetical crossroads. *Religious Education*, 59, 145-149.

Smart, James D. (1969). *The quiet revolution: The radical impact of Jesus on men of his time*. Philadelphia: Westminster.

Smith, Francis W. (1916). *Jesus--Teacher: Principles of education for both public and Bible school teachers*. New York: Sturgis & Walton.

Sorensen, Norman D. (1953). *How Christ used questions*. Unpublished Th.M. thesis, Dallas Theological Seminary.

Squires, Walter A. (1927). *The pedagogy of Jesus in the twilight of to-day*. New York: George Doran.

Stanton, Graham M. (1974). *Jesus of Nazareth in New Testament preaching*. Cambridge: Cambridge University Press.

Stanton, Graham M. (1977). Presuppositions in New Testament criticism. In I. Howard Marshall (Ed.), *New Testament interpretation: Essays on principles and methods*, pp. 60-71. Grand Rapids, MI: Eerdmans.

Stein, Robert H. (1978). *The method and message of Jesus' teachings*. Philadelphia, PA: Westminster.

Stemple, F. W. (1961). Qualities of the "master teacher." *Educational Forum*, 25, 227-231.

Stevens, George B. (1901). *The teaching of Jesus.* New York: Macmillan. (reprinted 1929)

Sweet, J. P. M. (1984). The Zealots and Jesus. In Ernst Bammel & C. F. D. Moule (Eds.), *Jesus and the politics of his day*, pp. 1-9. Cambridge: Cambridge University Press.

Swete, Henry B. (1904). *Studies in the teaching of our Lord* (2nd ed.). London: Hodder & Staughton.

Tannehill, Robert C. (1975). *The sword of his mouth.* Philadelphia: Fortress. (SBL Semeia Supplements No. 1).

Taylor, Vincent (1955). *The life and ministry of Jesus.* London: Macmillan.

Tipsword, Harrison M. (1916). *The pedagogics of Jesus.* Boston: Badger.

Toynbee, Arnold (Ed.) (1969). *The crucible of Christianity: Judaism, Hellenism, and the historical background to the Christian faith.* New York: World Publishing Company.

Trocme, Etienne (1973). *Jesus as seen by his contemporaries.* Philadelphia: Westminster.

Turner, E. W. (1963). *Historicity and the gospels: A sketch of historical method and its application to the gospels.* London: Mowbray.

Tyler, Ralph W. (1949). *Basic principles of curriculum and instruction.* Chicago: University of Chicago Press.

Van Wagnen, Oliver (1911). The pedagogy of Jesus. *Education*, 32, 169-176.

Vermes, Geza (1973). *Jesus the Jew: A historian's reading of the Gospels.* London: Collins.

Voegtle, Anton (1971). The miracles of Jesus against their contemporary background. In Hans J. Schultz (Ed.), *Jesus in his time*, pp. 98-105. London: SPCK.

Walter, Kaspar (1976). *Jesus the Christ.* London: Burns & Oates.

Weigle, Luther A. (1939). *Jesus and the educational method.* New York: Abingdon.

Wendt, Hans H. (1892). *The teaching of Jesus* (2 vols.). Edinburgh: T. & T. Clark.

Wilder, Amos N. (1971). *Early Christian rhetoric: The language of the gospel.* Cambridge, MA: Harvard University Press.

Wilson, Carl (1976). *With Christ in the school of disciple building: A study of Christ's method of building disciples.* Grand Rapids, MI: Zondervan.

Wilson, Clifford A. (1975). *Jesus: The master teacher.* Grand Rapids, MI: Baker (reprint of *Jesus the teacher*, 1974).

Winter, Paul (1971). Sadduccees and Pharisees. In Hans J. Schultz (Ed.), *Jesus in his time*, pp. 47-56, London: SPCK.

Winterowd, W. Ross (Ed.) (1975). *Contemporary rhetoric: A conceptual background with readings.* "Introduction," pp. 1-37. New York: Harcourt, Brace Jovanovich.

INDEX

22168763R00128

Printed in Poland
by Amazon Fulfillment
Poland Sp. z o.o., Wrocław